DragonRising Publi

The StressFish Guide To
EmoTrance

Written by
Dr T.E. Lynch

1st Edition 2011

The StressFish Guide to EmoTrance

© 2011 Teresa Lynch

ISBN 978-1-908269-02-7

First Edition

Published by

DragonRising Publishing

The Starfields Network Ltd.

45 Gildredge Road

Eastbourne

East Sussex

BN21 4RY

United Kingdom

www.DragonRising.com

Printed and bound in Great Britain by
CPI Antony Rowe, Chippenham and Eastbourne

Other Energy Healing Titles:

The StressFish Guide to Easy EFT by Silvia Hartmann

EmoTrance: Emotions, Energy, Information and Love
    by Silvia Hartmann

The EmoTrance Yearbook

Tapping for Kids by Angie Muccillo

The StressFish Guide To
EmoTrance

Praise for The StressFish Guide to EmoTrance:

I tremendously enjoyed reading "Stressfish Guide to EmoTrance," by Dr. Teresa Lynch. It was stimulating, informative, and very well written. Providing basic, easy-to-follow instructions on participating in exercises to enhance and reinforce the learning of EmoTrance was a wonderful bonus. I commend Dr. Lynch in her effort and success in providing us with this wonderful tool with which we are able to help ourselves attain good emotional and physical health.

Roni Michaels-DeBlank, MSW, LCSW

Bravo Terry! This book is self-empowering! You have captured the essence of what we all need to do when we have "stuck energy"... just let it "soften and flow". It's simply brilliant! As we give our bodies the "attention" it needs by using "intention" we can take control and heal ourselves forever...it's only energy! EmoTrance is a wonderful complement with EFT. I recommend adding this wonderful energy technique to your grab bag!

Annie Siegel,
Certified EFT Practitioner and Certified Hypnotherapist
www.roadtoemotionalfreedom.com

Stress is a "life limiter".

Are you tired of just "hanging in there"?
Do you want to take your life to a
completely different dimension?

Are you ready to transform your stress from
states of confusion, despair, anger or fear to
those of love and joy?

Welcome to EmoTrance.

Contents

The Mission Statement xii

PART I EmoTrance

Introduction 3

My Story 6

What is EmoTrance?. 12

    EmoTrance Basics 13

    Taking a Closer Look at Stress 13

    How Does EmoTrance Help?. 14

    The Effects of Stress: *Energioso Stuckitis* 15

    Energioso Stuckitis! 16

    Energy Nutrition. 17

        The Vitamins and Minerals
          of Energy Nutrition 18

    Movement and De-Stressing. 20

    The Experience of EmoTrance 21

        Time to Pause: The Wall 25

    Steps of EmoTrance 27

        Step 1: Where Do You Feel This
          in Your Body? 29

        Step 2: Show Me With Your Hands 29

        Step 3: How Does the Energy Feel? 31

        Step 4: Where Else in Your Body
          Do You Feel This? 32

        Step 5: Where Does the Energy Want
          to Go? 32

        Step 6: Soften and Flow 32

        Step 7: Re-assess, Repeat, Release (RRR) 33

        Time to Pause: Reducing Heightened Stress . . 34

PART II **Falling in Flow With You: EmoTrance**
and Daily Living

Introduction 38

How to Use This Section 39

   Add a Few EmoTrance Activities to Your Day . . . 40

      Greeting the Day 40

      Greeting the Night 41

   EmoTrance Activities for Flowing Energy

      Drawing in Energies 44

      Have a Nice Day 45

   EmoTrance Activities to Manage Stress

      Insults .46

      Compliments 48

      Energy Shower 50

      Letting Go of Shields 52

      Using Your Healing Hands 54

      Healing Hands and a Partner 57

   Movement and EmoTrance

      The Stretch 58

      Energy Dancing 59

      Jogging 61

   Reflection Tools to Bring Healing Moments

      Heart Healing 62

      Attitude of Gratitude 63

      Practicing Self-Compassion 65

   Conclusion 67

PART III   **EmoTrance in Action**

         Case Histories 70

              An EmoTrance Experience: Flight Anxiety 71

                    Time to Pause: Relieving Anxiety 75

                    Time to Pause: Experiencing Finer Energy
                        and Learning to Follow with Intention . . . 76

              An EmoTrance Experience: Releasing
              Past Anger 78

                    Time to Pause: Releasing Anger 87

              An EmoTrance Experience: Nurses and
              Their Desire to Know More 89

                    Time to Pause: Emotional Healing. 95

              An EmoTrance Experience: A Sixth Grade
              Class: Math Test Anxiety and Problems
              with Bullies 96

                    Time to Pause: Relieving Stress 101

         Closing 102

PART IV   **References and Resources** 108

         About the Author 115

FIGURES

         Figure 1 EmoTrance is An Energy Bridge. 22

         Figure 2 The SUE Scale 23

         Figure 3 The Steps of EmoTrance. 28

MISSION STATEMENT

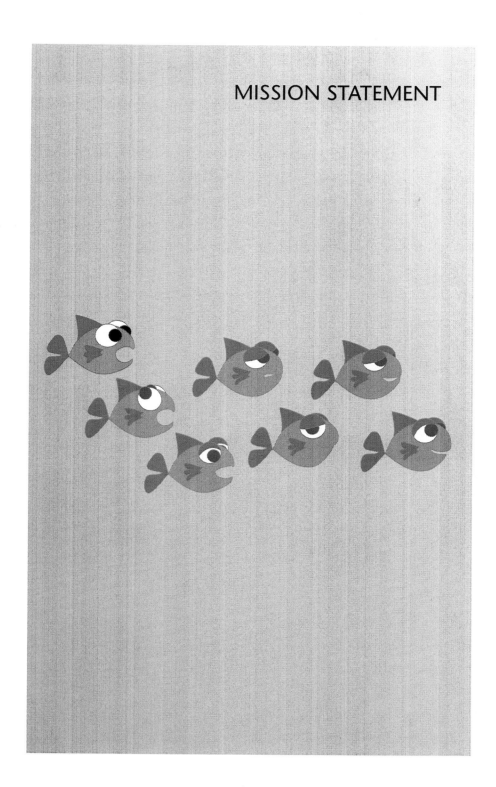

The Mission Statement

There is too much stress in the world!

The word "stress" is being bandied about everywhere and we hear it so much we have gotten used to it and accept it as something that's to be expected in this day and age.

Stress can even be a good thing under certain circumstances—right?

WRONG!

Stress is a TERRIBLE thing!

"Stress is a terrible thing!"

Stress…

- destroys enjoyment of life,
- erodes health,
- causes people to make truly stupid decisions and act in crazy and unpredictable ways.

Stress leads to emotional disturbances that can

- ruin the lives of whole families,
- and whole businesses;
- stress causes illness,
- get in the way of sex, intimacy and love,
- keep people in poverty, misery and desolation,
- create anger, rage, depression and madness,
- and is nothing short of a true SCOURGE of human existence.

We at StressFish.com are convinced that people can't ever be all they were meant to be whilst they are being driven crazy by stress—so we've decided to do something about it.

**We want to actively help to
REDUCE STRESS in the world!**

Every person who learns how to de-stress in their lives is going to be less stressed.

That means practically that they will be nicer—friendlier, more compassionate, more patient, **more loving**—to their colleagues, to their clients, their employees, their family, their friends, and even total strangers in the street.

Every person who learns how to take control of their stress and understand what that is and how it affects us, steps into a position of making better decisions, inventing less crazy systems, making less mistakes and doing better work all around.

**Stressed people can't
see the bigger picture.**

Stress causes tunnel vision and extreme emotions, which then drive destructive and downright stupid ideas and decisions on all levels—whether this is the decision to start using crack, or whether it is the decision that a few dollars on the bottom line of an already super rich company are more important than the well being of Planet Earth, or the humans who have to live and work here.

**We believe in people, and in the fact that
people CAN make good decisions, have good lives,
and are in essence, GOOD PEOPLE—as long as
they're not stressed out of their minds!**

With our best wishes,
The Team
http://www.StressFish.com

Part I
EMOTRANCE

Introduction

Have you ever had the opportunity to sit and watch the movement of fish in an aquarium? It can be mesmerizing. The hypnotic nature of simply staring at the undulating fish may take you to a place within that is calm and serene. Maybe even to a place filled with joy or pleasure as a smile comes to your face...all this occurring while the world around you remains chaotic. You are guided by the simple action of the movement of fish into a place of reduced stress: thus Stressfish.

I wrote *The Stressfish Guide to EmoTrance* in the hopes that it will fulfill the meaning of its title by guiding you into a world of less stress by teaching you how to move your own body's energies through your energy system using a simple tool called EmoTrance.

Although an aquarium can provide a wonderful form of stress relief, you cannot put it in your back pocket. EmoTrance is a modality that you can take wherever you go and, once incorporated into your life, can be an amazing tool for stress relief anytime, anywhere!

No matter how you look at it, stress is everywhere. Open a newspaper, go on-line, turn on the TV and you will receive constant stress-filled messages. Even if you are practicing techniques to reduce your stress,

"EmoTrance is a truly fantastic system for brightening all our spirits and experiencing life in a whole new way."
—Silvia Hartmann

there are times when it is nearly impossible *not* to get overwhelmed by the amount of information available to you on-line, the number of emails you have to answer, and the amount of technology that is available at your finger tips. As you are attempting to manage all that, you may need to drive to work, take your children to their events, struggle with finances, try to maintain healthy relationships...and don't forget to eat right! You go to bed, wake up, and it starts all over again. Stress is unavoidable.

As a health professional, I have treated a variety of different patients over the years. I have taught students in the field of physical therapy at both the college and the university levels. In my profession, I have witnessed the countless detrimental effects stress can have on the lives of my patients, students, family members, friends, and, of course, on myself.

Because of my own quest for personal well-being, I have always been interested in looking for ways to heal myself from the effects of stress and other problems that may arise in my body. This quest has also filled my desire to learn, grow, and upgrade my skills as a member of the healing professions. When I find something that works for me, I make it my life's purpose to bring it to others.

My search for healing has brought me on a journey that has come full circle. Initially, there was a part of me that had disconnected from my body, trusting that others knew more about my body than *me*! Now I believe in the innate wisdom of my own body. I *truly* believe that God would not create something that could not heal itself through the *very* Source that created it. For it to be otherwise would not be a very good prototype! But that's me. Research body wisdom for yourself and you will discover the emphasis placed on the ability of our bodies to communicate to us on many different levels. Tapping into that wisdom has been a way for me to heal. Over the years my passion has shifted from a mechanistic view of the body to exploring modalities that help me connect with my inner body wisdom and its ability to heal.

EmoTrance is one of those leading modalities that does exactly what I had been looking for! EmoTrance has brought me to a place that connects to both my inner healer and my inner body wisdom. While practicing EmoTrance, I believe I have not only received emotional healing but physical healing as well. In the simplicity of this technique, EmoTrance has gently guided me into flowing away the negative emotions—stress and anxiety—and transforming them to joy, love, and well-being.

I want to live the best life I can, filled with an abundance of health, wealth, and happiness. I am sure you do too. My first goal in writing this book was to let you know there are new systems and methods for achieving the health and well-being you desire. These new modalities are effective and can be life changing. This help is simple and affordable. It's something you can learn on your own time in the comfort of your home.

This book is written in three parts, each of which is designed to stand alone or that can be read in sequence. The first section highlights some of the key concepts of EmoTrance along with the main steps to follow. The second section will guide you through exercises to add to your daily EmoTrance experience. In the last section, several real-life scenarios are presented to further your knowledge and experience of EmoTrance in action.

When you are looking at new techniques in stress management, EmoTrance is a must. With practice, it can absolutely transform your life!

My Story

In 1994, I was diagnosed with Multiple Sclerosis. There was no cure. I was devastated.

I asked "Why me? What could cause this?"

My doctor mentioned that one of the factors that could bring on Multiple Sclerosis was stress. That resonated with me immediately because at that time I was leading a very stressful life. I was teaching at a major university, treating patients, serving my community, and raising a family.

Stress. It can be crippling. It can be a killer.

The major treatment for Multiple Sclerosis was medication. I chose not to go in that direction. Deep within me, I knew there had to be something else, something more. I knew I needed to change the way I lived my life, and I certainly needed to better manage my stress!

I was in the middle of experiencing a flare up of Multiple Sclerosis when my sister sent me a book by Louise Hay called, *You Can Heal Your Life*. I found the book challenging and revolutionary. It introduced me to the powerful concept that it could be my very thoughts that had helped to create my illness.

At first, I found this insulting! But, as I examined my thoughts I found them to be filled with negativity of self: anxiety, worry, shame, and embarrassment if something should go wrong. Certainly there were good thoughts here and there, but the self-deprecating thoughts ruled. I had taken on so many pressures and unrealistic beliefs of what I should be and do, no wonder I was overwhelmed. It is no wonder I was "stressed out". My thoughts would make anyone sick!

I began the process of taking responsibility for my thoughts and the way I thought by putting together affirmations I said to myself daily. I was excited by the results that simply changing my thinking brought to my overall health. I was eating more nutritiously, getting more exercise, and feeling a higher connection to spirit.

I still had Multiple Sclerosis.

Yet, from the moment I started feeling better from using the affirmations in Louise Hay's book, I knew I was on the right track. I also knew there was more.

I became passionate about searching for ways to heal from this disease and it brought me on an inner journey that would shape my life from that moment on. After many years, this journey would lead me to EmoTrance.

Before the discovery of EmoTrance, my research brought me to Energy Medicine, Energy Psychology, Reiki and other modalities, all of which played an important part in my healing journey. The major gift of these modalities was in understanding the role of the energy system in each person and feeling that energy move through the body.

Coming from the medical model, I did not know the energy system existed as an important aspect in patient care. It was not part of my formal education. Yet now, in my quest for a cure for my illness, the energy system and its connection to my inner spirit became the key to unlocking a door to a whole new path to healing. I was very excited with the results I was getting when I used energy work for both my clients and myself.

Yet, I still felt there was a piece missing. In the course of my recovery I had this feeling of tightness in my throat and chest that was unexplainable. While surfing the internet in 2008, I began reading about EmoTrance. I knew I had found something truly extraordinary. I delved into the book by Dr. Silvia Hartmann, *Oceans of Energy*, and this directed me to the next level in my healing process.

Do you know what made the EmoTrance technique so beautiful? It was simple.

Although I knew my thoughts and emotions were connected, the book taught me how important my emotions were in relationship to my energy body. For example, I learned that my emotions are the feedback mechanism of the energy body and that if I treated the energy body, my emotions would change. This was another revolutionary concept for me and it made sense, but it didn't stop there! When I felt the pressure within when I was feeling angry or sad, the location of that pressure was where the actual damage to my energy system was occurring!

This resonated deeply with me. It just made sense—and in a very loving and practical way as well. Through EmoTrance, I was able to "soften and flow" the energy in my throat and chest and for the first time in years, I felt wonderful inside and out.

Little did I know then how powerful my "thinking" was, along with the "emotions" they created in the management of my stress and overall health. I did not then know about how my stored or suppressed "emotions" could form "energy blockages" that my body experienced as stress and disease. I discovered that I could release stress simply by my intention to do so. EmoTrance was amazing and it was simple.

What astonished me the most was that I could feel the energy move, leaving or dissipating from my body. I never knew I could feel that. I never knew I could move energy within me. I always had the ability, I just never knew it! Letting go began to have a whole new meaning for me when connected to the flow of energy.

EmoTrance awakened my "inner healer". As these energy blockages were released, the flow of energy moving through me brought a heightened sense of love, joy and well-being. EmoTrance was the missing piece in my healing journey!

For the first time since I was diagnosed, I began to feel in control over something I had been told was "uncontrollable". After incorporating EmoTrance into my life and flowing energy through me, I have come to truly believe I no longer have Multiple Sclerosis!

My overall purpose in writing this book was to share with you the journey of EmoTrance in my life and to give you this amazing tool that may be the missing piece in your puzzle of life. The piece that could awaken your "inner healer" as it did mine, the piece that can free you from the emotional distress everyday living can bring and give you the freedom to flow with life in a spirit of love, joy and ongoing emotional transformation.

Now, how about you? What kind of stressors are you experiencing? Are you feeling sad, overwhelmed, worried? Are you just longing for some peace in your life? Are you in need of healing from emotional wounds? Well, you are not alone.

Stress is a "life limiter". It reduces you to limited thinking, ideas, possibilities, etc. It immobilizes energy levels, causing fatigue and feelings of not being able to do one more thing! You feel like you are barely surviving, getting by, or just "hanging in there".

Are you tired of just "hanging in there" and want to take your life to a whole different dimension? Are you ready to transform your stress from states of confusion, despair, anger, or fear to those of peace and joy? Then, welcome to one of the most fascinating healing modalities of our century; a modality that is simple to use and gets you in touch with your inner self—or more specifically, your inner healer.

Welcome to EmoTrance

Created in 2002 by Silvia Hartmann, a well-known innovator and pioneer in energy therapies, EmoTrance is emerging as an "indispensable tool for releasing worry, sadness, and fear and generally helping with relationships and love pain, past hurts, and other emotional wounds" (S. Topham, Finding the River, pg. 111).

Simple and easy to grasp, anyone can learn EmoTrance and at almost any age. With this tool you can experience the flow of life in ways you never thought possible. You will be given an avenue of release to the repetitive emotional challenges that otherwise would continue to pile up inside your body, causing undo stress.

Today you have the capacity to be in control of your healing and of relieving your stress on many different levels, especially on an emotional level. Why? Because it is *your* body, *your* spirit, and *your* mind. They are unique to you and no one else. Breakthroughs in emotional healing, like EmoTrance, may change the way you look at healing your brokenness, relieving your stress, and maintaining your wholeness by understanding the movement of energy within you.

As Silvia Hartmann stated in her first book on EmoTrance, *Oceans of Energy*, "EmoTrance is...a device designed to help us relearn the ways of the Oceans of Energy, for us to repair ourselves with volition and prepare ourselves for a true opening to what there really is, all around us, all the time."

What does it mean to re-learn? It means the ability to flow your body's healing energy. There is nothing to seek; it is already there, waiting to be awakened. EmoTrance empowers you to discover and recognize the healing flow of energy that has always been within you. It is a wonderful yet simple way of becoming more aware of your own energy.

If you have picked up this book, you are probably feeling stressed, anxious, depressed, or any range of emotions that brings a person to say, "Enough. I want to live the life I have always dreamed of! I am starting today to bring myself to that place of creativity and joy!"

Learning to flow the energy of distress within the body is a powerful life-changing experience and leads to a new way of being. You may never think, see, or feel life the same way again. EmoTrance changed my life. It is a process, though, and does take time and practice.

Keep in mind that the thoughts presented here may challenge your belief systems. For me, this has been an enlightening process. If this process resonates with you and speaks to you at some deep level, continue to move forward and be patient with yourself. Spend a moment in appreciation for taking time with your inner self.

If this process does not resonate with you and you feel it conflicts at some deeper level with where you need to go in your healing process, honor that in yourself. Do not take as truth something that is presented to you unless it resonates with you as truth on some level. Spend a moment in appreciation for taking the time to explore something new and different for yourself. Knowing what doesn't work is just as important as knowing what does.

Wherever you are in your quest for healing, stress relief, and truth, you are taking steps to change your life.

Thank you for exploring EmoTrance for stress relief. You have come to the right place.

> **Emotional Transformation**
>
> **Emo → Trans**
>
> **Emo → Trance**
>
> **EmoTrance**

What is EmoTrance?

The name EmoTrance is derived from the first syllables of the words emotional transformation and, thus, brings a profound healing experience by doing exactly what its name implies. EmoTrance is the technique of transforming negative emotions of deep hurt, anger, resentment, or fear to those of joy, love and happiness.

This transformational process occurs through learning how to *flow* your body's own energies through your energy body. This skill *cannot* be underestimated. It is an amazing tool to have and can alter your life!

EmoTrance recognizes that it is your lack of knowledge of your innate ability to flow energy that is largely responsible for the experience of stress and negative feelings in your life. Negative emotions get stuck in your body when they are *not* flowing through and released naturally.

Your body needs to do something with this stuck emotional energy and wants to communicate that to you in the form of emotional pain, physical pain, weight issues, illness, and others.

For example, let's take stress on the body in the form of emotional pain. At the point of emotional pain, what EmoTrance focuses on is:

- locating stuck emotional energy,
- placing full attention on that energy,
- using intention to allow the energy to flow, and
- flowing the energy until it is experienced in a happier, more vibrant way.

How EmoTrance encourages the energy to flow is remarkably simple—through using guiding words and your *intention*.

EmoTrance Basics

Let us try the EmoTrance process in its basic form.

- Breathe and relax your eyes:
- Think of a stressful situation.
- Ask yourself, "Where do I feel this in my body?"
- Bring your hands to the location of that feeling.
- Place your full attention there and say to the area, "Soften and flow."

Continue this process by using the intention of "soften and flow" to give permission for the energy to leave. This is not accomplished in a *"willful"* way but in a form of *"letting go,"* with simply your desire for the energy to flow.

This is EmoTrance. (We will look more in depth at the process in the section on "Steps to EmoTrance".)

You may be thinking, "How am I going to get to emotional transformation when there is *so* much stress in my life? Where would I even begin?"

With the stressors you are experiencing in your life, take a moment to think of where you *feel* that in your body. What emotions are contributing to your stress? These are the emotions you would focus on first when using EmoTrance.

Taking a Closer Look at Stress

Let's take a moment to examine the connection that stress has to your life and what EmoTrance is and can do relative to that stress.

When you are in a stressful situation, your focus tends to be on the situation that is causing your stress (which, of course, makes sense). Your focus is *intent* on a problem which exists *outside* of you. It may be a problem that you are trying to take control of and you think if you did things differently, or if people or circumstances where different, things would change in your favor.

If you look at the *intent* or intention, with the popular phrase, "what you focus on expands," you are only going to get more of the same!

In other words, your stress results from trying to control something from the outside. Meanwhile, on the inside, you feel things are *out of control* no matter how hard you try.

EmoTrance turns this around, because the truth is, you have *no* control over things outside of you. You think you do, but you don't. Herein lies the conflict. Your stress is arising from trying to take control over something that is external that is not yours to control. It is life in process.

What you do have control over is your internal response to life; this is where EmoTrance comes in.

$$\text{Stress} = \text{the process of control from the outside in} + \text{energy block}$$

$$\text{EmoTrance} = \text{the process of control from the inside out} + \text{energy flow}$$

How Does EmoTrance Help?

EmoTrance gently invites you to explore your inner energies and then takes you to a space where you can look at the world differently. In a stressful situation, EmoTrance is a tool that gives you control from the inside out.

EmoTrance redirects the focus within, where you experience the energy or *sensations* that are being generated by your thoughts about the problem. EmoTrance takes your attention off the outside problems and thoughts and focuses it solely on the sensations. These sensations are a form of energy *stored* in your body. Stored energy is stuck energy or blocked energy, and energy, by its very nature, needs to flow. Stuck energy is the beginning of the uneasiness you are experiencing. Over time the constant build up of stuck energy can lead to disease in some instances (which was so in my case).

By flowing the energies surrounding the problem—the thoughts, feelings and emotions—you are now internally releasing any hold the problem may have on you. As you continue to flow the energy and feel the positive effects of free-flowing energy, you may begin to experience the gift I have experienced with EmoTrance: having control over what was thought to be uncontrollable.

You do not have control over what happens outside of you, but you do have control over what happens inside of you. What is bizarre here is that control comes from *letting go* of stuck energy within your energy body. Actually, the only control that you have is the "yes" you say to letting go and letting the energy flow.

> *"The more willing you are to surrender to the energies within you, the more power can flow through you."*
> —*Shakti Gawain*

You know when your body's energies are flowing because you feel energetic, vibrant, excited about life, and joyful, or what Silvia Hartmann calls the *Even Flow*. This is the state we were born to live in. It is our birthright!

The Effects of Stress: Energioso Stuckitis

How can you tell if you are not in *Even Flow*? If you do not have enthusiasm, vitality, enjoyment for simply being you, then you have stuck energy somewhere within you!

To emphasize the detrimental effects of stress, I have created a new diagnosis for all the sensations and emotions arising from stress (mind you, that is just about everything) and it is:

Energioso Stuckitis!

In the word *Stuckitis*, the suffix "-itis" is Greek in derivation and means inflammation. The increased sensations in our bodies from stress resulting from this inflammation can be experienced as emotional pain in the form of anger and depression. There is evidence in current research that connects negative emotions with disease processes. For instance, anger has been linked to chronic inflammation in the body.

The "-oso" at the end of energy is Spanish for bear and is a reminder that stress is a reaction of the sympathetic nervous system in a response called "fight, flight or freeze" (fff), which is the body's way of reacting to perceived threats or danger. The "fff" response is an innate survival instinct that is part of our evolutionary heritage and evolved as a way to protect us from predators.

For example, if you were about to be attacked by a bear, you would have instinctively either fought or taken flight. If that wasn't working, you might have frozen and played dead to fool the bear or saber tooth tiger or whatever predator may have be attacking you. Phrases like, "I was scared stiff," represent the freeze response.

The problem today is that the nervous system has not adapted over the millenniums to the changing stressors of our current society. It inappropriately still thinks that when you are under stress, you are being attacked by a bear.

So your boss tells you that you have just been "let go" and your nervous system responds, "Bear!" You are in traffic and late for a meeting and your nervous system responds, "Bear!" You are having an argument with your spouse, you cannot pay your bills, you locked your keys in the car—"Bear! Bear! Bear!" You get the idea.

Your nervous system responds to any attack to your person by releasing the hormones adrenalin and cortisol to protect you. Adrenalin and cortisol are designed to speed up your heart rate and slow down digestion in order to give you a boost of energy and strength so you can respond to danger. Constant release of adrenalin and cortisol in a society where stress is chronic creates damage to your body over time.

EmoTrance does *not* directly influence the physiology behind stress, but it *is* designed to give you a modality to assist in releasing the emotions arising from a stressful situation. EmoTrance is a tool to help prevent *Energioso Stuckities* by going within and identifying the sensations backing up in the energy system and releasing them into the world. EmoTrance effects *only* the energy flow in the energy body and, with practice, can transform negative emotional responses to stress into those of well-being and joy.

Ultimately, EmoTrance is all about *you*—your emotions, releasing your stress, and the flowing of energy in, through, around, and about you. As you learn this technique and practice it regularly, you will begin to experience a fullness to life that you have always longed for even if you have only recently realized it was missing.

The EmoTrance technique itself is simple. The amazing part is that when you transform the emotional experience within you, you transform your experience or perception of the world outside you.

As you regularly flow energy, you come to see the world with a new set of eyes. Your perception changes and things and tasks that seemed monumental, now become the building blocks of a life unfolding around you.

Energy Nutrition

If you have been struggling with a stressful life, you may be lacking the energy nutrition that your energy body needs.

The evolution of what EmoTrance calls the "energized end state" is the ability to draw energy into yourself from just about anything or anyone in your environment. Once the energy is drawn in, it can then be flowed through your energy system and back out into the world. EmoTrance calls this "energy nutrition". It is a powerful concept.

When you research energy nutrition on-line, the majority of the information you will find speaks about food and the energy or fatigue caused by certain foods. Yes, what foods you eat are important, but this is not the nutrition to which EmoTrance refers.

Just as it is important for your body to receive nourishment from different foods to maintain good physical health, EmoTrance recognizes your energy body and its energy system needs nourishment from not only food but also the unlimited energy sources available outside of you. And just as the physical body needs food to be taken in, processed and passed back out into the environment through the digestive tract (and we all know what happens when food gets backed up in the body!), so the energy body needs to do the same with energy.

"Energy forms cannot be stored and must come in fresh, again and again, every day for optimal functioning of the energy system."

—S. Hartmann

Energy sources include music, animals, landscapes, plants, other people (this is by far the most important); the list is unending. These energy sources can nourish your system and heighten your awareness of the world around you, bringing more love and light into your life.

The Vitamins and Minerals of Energy Nutrition

Just think, if you are feeling a little anxious and depressed, the energy nourishment of a phone call to a vitamin BFF (text for best friends forever), may be just the nutrition you are missing!

What if boredom is ruling your life and you feel you are dragging yourself to get places? Maybe a little vitamin A (for *adventure*) is just what your energy system needs! Take a hike in the mountains or along the water front or explore a nearby town. Better yet, take a friend with you.

Feeling a little lonely or lacking in purpose? Take an energetic boost of vitamins C and N (for *caring* and *nurturing*) by volunteering for a local cause or reaching out to someone in need. Gardening is another great way to get a dose of vitamins C and N. You may be surprised at how taking action can help make a difference in your energy diet.

Watching the sunrise and experiencing the dawning a new day may be packed with enough of the energetic vitamins and minerals of wonder, awe, serenity and bliss to last you for a few days! Just remember that too much of any vitamin may cause problems; know the right balance for you!

Ultimately, when we are speaking of energy nutrition, we want the energy of love to prevail in our lives. A good dose of the unconditional love of a pet may lift your spirits at the end of a long day or reaching out to others with kindness may bring a circle of love right back to you.

It is important to note that when you have heightened moments of energy nutrition, sometimes you may not want to let go of them. However, it is important not to store up energy, whether it is good or bad. Energy needs to flow in, through, and out of you, cleansing and nourishing your system. For example, you witness the most magnificent sunrise and try to capture it in pictures. Instead, let go—that energy needs to flow in, through, and out of you. You "fell in love" for the first time—let go, that energy needs to flow in, through, and out of you. Your energy system needs constant nourishment with fresh new energy on a daily basis or otherwise your system will become stagnant or backed up. (But don't worry if energy does get stuck now and then. You can get it flowing again because you have EmoTrance now!)

Thus, as you look for ways to relieve your stress and maintain feelings of well-being in your life, energy nutrition is a vital component. Fortunately, it is everywhere to be found. So, take a moment and go touch a tree, listen to music, or simply look into the eyes of another.

Movement and De-Stressing

Physically moving your body is a wonderful way to get energy to flow. Combining that movement with EmoTrance can be a powerful stress reliever. EmoTrance can awaken your "inner feeler". As you move, you place your attention inside and you become aware of the release of energy through your body. Feel the give and take of energy flow as you stretch, walk, and move about.

Moshe FeldenKrais stated, "Movement is life." We can go on to say that energy is movement and that energy needs to move and flow and be a constant expression of life in action.

If you are experiencing overwhelming stress and there is an incredible amount of stuck energy in your body, get up and move! Go for a walk, breath in deeply, turn on music that inspires you and dance...or simply go outside. Find some form of movement you enjoy whether it is yoga or gardening or playing an instrument, etc. Move! It is a great stress reliever and provides plenty of energy nutrition for your energy body. And just as movement helps your physical body's digestive system to flow, it does the same for the body's energy system.

Do not worry if you do not like to "exercise". Exercise may be a word that has come to add to your stress. "You better exercise!" "You are not getting enough exercise!" "If you don't exercise your bad cholesterol will go up!" Just writing this makes my stress level go up (and I love exercise)!

EmoTrance IS Experiential

The gift here is simply to *move*. Learn again the love you had for movement when you were a child exploring and moving about. Go out and look at children playing and get inspired. Exercise has regulated movement to just another routine and for many it simply lacks inspiration.

Do you want to de-stress?

- Stretch slowly, pause and feel the tingle of energy flow through you.
- Get up and dance.
- All the movement you need may be just inside of you.
- And breathe! After all, it is the source of all movement.

(For more about Energy Movement, there is the Energy Dancing Activity in Part II of this book.)

The Experience of EmoTrance

EmoTrance is not something you can merely read about in a book or discuss with another in order to master its techniques; EmoTrance is experiential. It is something you need to do and feel.

We live in a world where people have disconnected from their energy systems, causing long-term emotional distress. In fact, this distress is a strong disconnect that is seen by the way we fear our very own bodies and the emotions and sensations they generate. For example, my female clients report they were told, "it is not right to get angry," and my male clients learned, "big boys don't cry". When things would go wrong in their lives (which is bound to happen!), shame and embarrassment would sweep through their bodies. They would try to suppress the emotions, wait it out, or hope the pain from the sensations they were experiencing

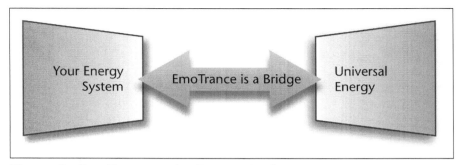

Figure 1   EmoTrance is An Energy Bridge.

would just go away. They were unaware of the fact that they were creating energy blockages within themselves.

EmoTrance is a bridge between individuals and the energy of the Universe (Figure 1). The technique can help you connect on a very individual level to healing energy. With EmoTrance, you become aware of the movement of your energy system and the key role it plays in emotional healing.

What is this flowing, healing energy all about? Where does the energy come from?

From everywhere. There is energy all around us to flow, in, through, and about us at any given time. For many the "source" of the energy takes the name of God or Universal Life Force (or whatever you connect with as true for you.) EmoTrance describes the source as the Creative Order and that whenever you assist *Even Flow* with your intention, the creative order is on your side.

Ultimately, when energy flows there is a healing of your spirit. In fact, EmoTrance Practitioners consider themselves "spirit specialists!"

Now, when everything flows well there is a feeling of *Even Flow*. Life is experienced as a vibrant energy with a presence of love in, about, and around you. All is well.

Yet, the sensation of *Energioso Stuckitis* can be very painful and the opposite of *Even Flow*. For example, have you ever been terribly hurt or experienced deep grief and felt that you were "drowning in your tears?" Or have you been in a situation where you have to speak up yet you feel as if something is lodged in your throat? Or you may have felt your stress rise so high that you thought you were going to "blow your top", and maybe you did.

EmoTrance has been developed to give you the tool to not only relieve the stress and give avenues for this intense energy to leave, but also to bring you to a higher place of being. EmoTrance is not satisfied with just going to a place of no pain that is seen in general health care. EmoTrance wants to take you to the other end of the scale; the place of love, joy and well-being.

The scale in Figure 2 is the Subjective Units of Experience (SUE) scale. The darker end of the scale up to point zero is what is known as the Subjective Units of Discomfort (SUDs). This scale is used mostly to measure the experience of pain up to a point of no pain.

The SUE scale was designed to demonstrate that there are levels of experience outside of just "no pain". Have you ever been asked by a medical professional, "On a scale from 0 to 10, with 0 being no pain and 10 being exuberant and filled with happiness, just how happy are you? How much love and joy are you experiencing in your life?" Probably not. That is not their job. The health system

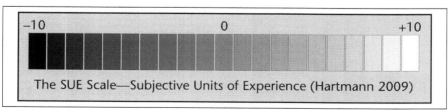

Figure 2 The SUE Scale

is not designed to do that and, of course, insurance will not cover beyond "no pain". But don't we all want someone to care about our level of happiness? This is where EmoTrance comes in.

Until EmoTrance, I would often ask my patients who were experiencing pain, "On a scale from 0 to 10, please describe the level of your pain to me with 0 being no pain and 10 being so much pain you could just cry." Whatever the patient's response, the overall goal was to get to a place of "no pain".That was very important. In our society, we are happy just to be in a place of "no pain"! Joy seems almost unattainable for many.

For example, after an EmoTrance session with a client who was in remission following surgery and treatment for breast cancer, we came to a place in the session where she was smiling, feeling a tingling sensation throughout her body and she stated, "I could just dance!" I asked her if the sensations she was experiencing could be described as "joy". She stopped, thought, looked at me and said, "I don't know, I haven't experienced joy in over nine years. I have forgotten what that feels like."

You may be thinking "how sad," but she just highlighted the two ends of the scale! If you do not know how to live on the other side of the scale, you would not know you are there even when it happens! It may even feel uncomfortable, but that is simply because it is unfamiliar. Again, you deserve to spend the majority of your time while you are here on this planet in a joy-filled state of being!

Your life is meant to receive from Source, to flow and give into the "Oceans of Energy". The cycle of giving and receiving becomes a wonderful continuum in the flow of life.

Everyone experiences EmoTrance in a different way because each person travels his or her own unique journey. In order for you to truly transform your emotional being, you must take time from the busy world you live in and find a place where you can be quiet. In this space you can give yourself the opportunity to expand and release the blocks your inner world has constructed; in other words, to do some emotional housekeeping!

It's almost like taking the remote while watching TV and pushing the pause button. When you press pause on the "program of life," you will have the opportunity to reflect and experience the process of EmoTrance. In this book, we will call the reflecting activities a "Time to Pause".

With practice you will also find that you can use EmoTrance at almost any moment or in any situation in which you find yourself, whether quiet or not. You will develop an instant built-in pause button.

As you practice EmoTrance and incorporate it into your life, you will be surprised to find that the inner and outer worlds start to meld together and a feeling of *oneness* occurs. This feeling of oneness often comes with a deep sense of joy or bliss; sometimes as a tingling feeling—the energized end state. This is an event to be cherished, reminding you of the beautiful energetic being that you are.

Time to Pause

The Wall

- Take a moment to relax and find a comfortable place to sit. Have a pen close by just in case you would like to jot down any thoughts that come to mind or anything you may feel in your body while you read along.
- Relax your eyes.
- Picture a wall, a great divide, where you stand on one side and your dreams are on the other. This wall is an incredible block, a hurdle to get over.
- Imagine the tool EmoTrance in the palm of your hands. You don't know what it can do for you yet, but you hold it trustingly and feel a surprising power within yourself.

- As you look at the wall, ask yourself, "Where do I feel it in my body? Where do I physically feel this divide in my body?"
- Place your hands where you can feel it and give it all of your attention.
- Now, extend your arms out and whisper to the wall, "Soften."
- To your surprise it does just that. It is softening.
- Now you whisper the word, "Flow," to the softening wall.
- The wall starts to dissolve. You lower your arms and wonder, "What is this magic I hold in my hands?"
- Pause: What are you experiencing now? Make a note if you feel anything in your body and where.
- Now you wander to what remains of the wall and whisper, "Where would you like to go, Wall?"
- The wall begins to dissolve away, through you and around you, joining the Oceans of Energy where it once was before and is now again.
- You look to see what was hiding behind the wall. There is a clean slate, a clean canvas drawing you forward and inviting you to start painting your life.
- You may feel a little excited or, possibly, a little afraid. Your thoughts have been so engrossed in the wall that you haven't had a moment to think of what life would be without it.
- Pause: Have you ever experienced this feeling? Where do you feel this in your body?
- You may even be slightly surprised that you actually miss the wall because it was so familiar.
- Pause: What would you miss about your wall?
- A voice within you says, "Let's paint...it's your time now."
- And you smile and say, "I am home."
- Pause: Take a moment and either write or just dream about what you would put on that canvas.
- What would your life look like with all the barriers/walls gone?

Steps of EmoTrance

In the previous Time to Pause, the basic steps of EmoTrance were introduced. For the moment, let us focus on the wall. What does the wall represent to you? You may have ideas in mind or you may have jotted down thoughts during the exercise. The wall is a part of your personal experience; something unique to you. Spend a moment in appreciation for taking that time for yourself.

Now, for the sake of learning EmoTrance, the wall represents blocked energy in you caused by negative emotions. This energetic block is caused by a thought, an event, or any memory that may have hurt or angered you resulting in a negative emotional response. This naturally adds to the experience of stress in your body.

The chart in Figure 3 shows the process of EmoTrance in emotional transformation. Do not worry about memorizing the steps of EmoTrance or doing it in the right order. You can't get it wrong! The steps and chart are there to meet a variety of learning styles.

On your journey to find ways to reduce your stress you may find difficult emotions arising that you may not have expected. Remember, you are the authority. At all times you must take care of yourself and do what is right for *you*. If the emotions resulting from the stress you are experiencing are too difficult, take the time to reach out to a health professional or an experienced EmoTrance practitioner to guide you along. Certified practitioners can be found through the EmoTrance website (www.EmoTrance.com).

Ready to begin? Here are the initial steps to follow in EmoTrance.

Tip: For this to be effective and to experience the release of energy within you, try to think of an instance where you felt a very high level of stress. Maybe you were extremely overwhelmed,

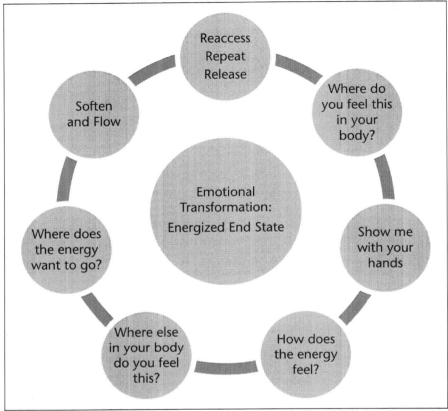

Figure 3 The Steps of EmoTrance.

in a state of panic, or felt deeply hurt or angered. An example from my experience is leaving my wallet behind at a grocery store and remembering it was there when I was 10 miles away! Several years ago, I had my four-year-old walking next to me in a department store. I turned and he was gone (hiding behind a display to play hide and seek) but that feeling in my chest would be an example of stuck energy. Other examples could be not being able to speak because you felt you had something lodged in your throat or being so angry and feeling the pressure rise in your head. Your example could be at the current moment or something that happened in your past. Do you have it? Once you do, try step 1.

Step 1: Where Do You Feel This in Your Body?

Take a moment to experience that sensation. What does it feel like? Where is it located? If you can feel it, if it is uncomfortable or painful, it is an injury that needs to be healed.

As discussed earlier, this is one of the fundamental concepts of EmoTrance. That place, that location in your body where you are feeling stress (i.e., where the stress sensation is the most physically uncomfortable), is an energy block or "stuck energy". How are you experiencing that stress? What are the emotions involved telling you of the status of your energy system?

Our emotions tell us how our energy system is doing at any given moment. They tell us what kind of shape it's in. This is the foundation of EmoTrance.

How simple is that? "Where do you feel that in your body?" Where you "feel" the emotional hurt or injury—the stress in your body—is the location of the actual damage to the energy system!

No guess work! I find this concept so simple yet so radical that I must repeat it for the sake of its brilliance.

(NOTE: Do not worry if you brought up a terrible emotional memory or other type of stress and you did not feel it in your body. This would be called a *shield* and will be discussed later. For the purpose of this exercise, try to pick a situation you can feel in your body.)

Step 2: Show Me With Your Hands

Place your hand or both hands over the location of the energy block or discomfort and give it all of your attention. For some people it is more comfortable to hold a hand above the area of the pain and not actually touch the body; just being close to the location is enough. If you are working with an EmoTrance Practitioner, they may need to have you show them the location of the injury with your hands so they may best assist you in releasing the block.

Explore this painful place or spot in your body caused by the recall of the unhappy memory or event that created your stress. Your energy system will let you know through your body that it needs attention and where. If you don't give the energy system the attention it needs to clear that block, it will eventually back up like a river hitting a damn until something bursts or just gives way.

Have you ever experienced a feeling that you where going to explode? Silvia Hartmann has likened this explosive feeling to a "pressure cooker". Your body was experiencing "stuck energy".

> *"All Emotions Are Cries Of Joy or Pain."*
> *—The Energy System, Silvia Hartmann*

Another thought to consider—energy is neither good nor bad. No matter how you are feeling, EmoTrance Practitioners would say, "It's only energy."

Yet, if the stuck, explosive energy is not addressed, how does it give way? Let's take a look at the totality: mind, body, and spirit. Through the mind, it can give way through judgmental thoughts, anger, extreme pressure like you are going to "loose it" or headaches and migraines.

Through your body it can give rise to abdominal problems, heart problems, joint problems, or other physical complaints.

Through your spirit, it shows up as sadness, anxiety and depression.

Thus, it is important to listen to the various forms of expression of energy in our bodies. Energy needs to move and flow and it will find a way to do so. You were never meant to hold onto it in the first place.

Oddly enough, the location of the stuck energy in your body can reveal the original energetic or emotional cause as well. For example, I had a client with neck pain and I asked her, "Who is a pain in your neck?" After discussing the particular individual which gave rise to her neck pain, we were able to flow the energy and the pain dissipated without doing anything more!

Step 3: How Does the Energy Feel?

In order to know if the energy is changing or dissipating, it is important to spend a moment with that energy to recognize its intensity and the strength of its block within you. To avoid confusion, EmoTrance does not use metaphors, but it does associate analogies with the states that

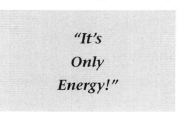

"It's Only Energy!"

water can take. For example, "the stuck energy I feel is as hard as ice," or, "it's murky," or, "it's dripping away".

And remember, no matter how painful it feels or how hurtful it is, remind yourself *it is only energy* and the nature of energy is that it needs to flow. This energy can be cleared and moved through the EmoTrance technique.

How comforting is that? Although the negative energy making up that emotion or sensation feels all encompassing, it is good to keep this statement as a reminder that you can heal.

It's only energy.

Step 4: Where Else in Your Body Do You Feel This?

While you take a moment to feel the intensity of the emotion and the energy block, explore within your body to see if there is anywhere else you are feeling a blockage from your emotional memory. From talking to many clients, I have found that when given a moment to check their bodies, they have often found evidence of energetic blocks, masked by the intensity of the original site of the injury, in other areas that were not at first apparent.

So take some time to investigate what you feel in your body. If you have scanned your body and don't feel a sensation of energy elsewhere, stay focused on the original site and pay attention to it. If you do feel a shift of the energy to another site, pay attention to that location and clear that area first with the following steps before returning to the site of the original injury and repeating the process.

Step 5: Where Does the Energy Want to Go?

As you pay attention to the stuck energy, you may notice that it has a direction it wants to go in order to leave your body. It is important to note that the energy can leave anywhere— out your nose, your toes, your finger, your ears, anywhere.

This question brings the intention of the "ability" of this stuck energy to flow and prepares the thought process for the possibility of its release from its original location. In other words, it brings to mind that the energy is meant to flow and that it can move.

Step 6: Soften and Flow

In this simple statement lies the power of our intention. We can simply tell the energy to leave. Not forcefully, but in a gentle, softening kind of a way.

Focus on the area of energy blockage and gently repeat, "Soften," to the energy. Tell the energy to, "Soften and flow." Now imagine the energy softening and flowing through you and moving out of you. Imagine the energy flowing out through energy pathways, no matter where they may be, until the energy flows all the way out. Again, let the energy flow follow whatever way or direction it needs to take until it is through and out.

When the energy starts to flow, just allow it to be. Try not to question how it is moving or why it may take a certain direction. Just trust that it is happening and give permission for it to do so.

Step 7: Re-assess, Repeat, Release (RRR)

Re-assess the process by recalling again the old emotion that gave rise to the emotional pain. Do this by returning to the place in your body where you first felt the energy block. Make a mental note of how it feels now. If there still is remaining energy there, repeat the process. Keep repeating the above steps, encouraging the energy to soften and flow, until the energy caused by the original memory releases quickly and smoothly and there is a very different feeling about you.

You know when you have released the energy block because you will feel either relieved, a tingling energy gently moving through your body, or a sense of simply feeling lighter. This is the "energized end-state".

The beauty of EmoTrance is its simplicity. You can enter the de-stressing process at any point and receive the benefits of EmoTrance. Just your desire to move the energetic block is sometimes enough to do so.

Time to Pause

Reducing Heightened Stress

Call your attention to a situation that creates a feeling of heightened stress in your body. Stay with the pressure sensation and perform the following steps:

- Where do you feel this in your body?
- Show me with your hands.
- How does the energy feel?
- Where else do you feel this in your body?
- Where does the energy want to go?
- Soften and Flow
- RRR

This is EmoTrance.

Make time for yourself. Take the "outer world pause" challenge. By doing so you will release the blocks, the *Energioso Stuckitis* holding back the river of life in you. In releasing the stuck energy, you will actually have more energy and a feeling of more time to do the things you want to do and to be the person you want to become!

Congratulations! You have learned a new tool called EmoTrance! Take a moment to honor yourself for doing so.

Let me emphasize that the basic technique of EmoTrance is simple. That's why Practitioners often say, "If it isn't simple, it is not EmoTrance."

Remember, there is no wrong way of doing this. Whenever you stop to connect with your inner energy being, it can only be good.

What if you forget the order of the steps? No problem. Wherever you enter into the EmoTrance technique, the process can work.

Simply taking the time to "feel" inward gets the energy system in motion. Your intention is a large part of the healing process.

And if you forget the steps, ask yourself what you do remember. EmoTrance can be as simple as:

- Where do I feel this in my body?
- Soften and flow

What if you have not felt the energy flow? Just being cognizant of your body and what you are feeling is a step in the right direction. Many of my clients tell me that after using EmoTrance for a period of time, all they have to do is say, "Soften and flow," and they feel better.

So congratulations again and enjoy the activities in the next section as a tool to enhance the gift of EmoTrance in your life.

Part II

FALLING IN FLOW WITH YOU:
EMOTRANCE AND DAILY LIVING

Introduction

Stress takes you out of the flow of life around you. "Falling in flow" is all about experiencing EmoTrance in yourself and the world you live in. The more you take opportunities to flow energy, the less stress you will feel. If you are flowing energy, it simply will not get stuck. This does not mean that you may never again get angry or loose patience with your child or someone you love, or that your workplace will suddenly change. Of course not! But those stressful situations will seem to happen much less.

There is a constant flow of energy. It never stops. Energy is everywhere leaving us so many ways to de-stress and nurture our energy bodies. There is so much energy to absorb; so much energy nutrition to be had!

Energy flows *in* you and *around* you. The activities in this section for "falling in flow" with the energy *around* you allows you to experience the EmoTrance process in nature, other people, and things in your life. The flowing of energy around and through your energy system feeds and nurtures it, giving it opportunities to evolve towards higher levels of well-being, bringing times of blissful living more frequently into your life.

Energy is everywhere and in everything. It is there for your taking to be

"Energy is everywhere and in everything.

It is there for our taking, to nourish us, to flow through us, to be enjoyed, to give back.

EmoTrance activities will heighten your energetic experiences for more fullness of life on this planet."

enjoyed. EmoTrance will heighten your energetic experiences for more fullness of life on this planet.

While doing the activities in this section, it is important for you to remember that EmoTrance is simple. If it is not simple, then it is not EmoTrance. Initially it may take time and practice, yes, but it is not "hard".

This may be a new experience for you because your life has probably been surrounded by "the hard". For example, when you learned something in school or learned new skills, it probably required intense concentration on the relevant facts and testing of some sort.

But EmoTrance is all about experiencing energy flow. It is more about the ability to relax, release stuck energy, receive the flow of energy that releasing brings, and allowing energy to flow through you from many different sources.

As you become familiar with adding EmoTrance to your life, you may create a few exercises of your own. The beauty of EmoTrance is that the more you practice the techniques, the less practice you will need because it will become a part of all you do.

How to Use This Section

So how do you "fall in flow with *you*?" There are several ways, and this section is divided into 5 areas that will help you to do that.

- Practice: add a few EmoTrance activities to your day.
- Gain a few techniques: manage stress and other daily problems you may face.
- Heal: use your healing hands with EmoTrance.
- Move: get moving with movement and EmoTrance with two activities to enjoy the energy that comes with active movement.

- EmoTrance Reflections: have a few tools on hand when you have time to bring healing moments to your body.

Each activity is designed to stand alone. You can choose any exercise and start right away and have fun! Each activity is preceded with a section called "A Thought" and followed by "The Basic Technique". These are included to help you get more out of the EmoTrance activity. At the end of each activity there is a reflection on the activity called, "Going Deeper". These are simply ideas and experiences I have had with each activity.

If you enjoy journaling, you may want to write about your experiences with these EmoTrance activities as well.

This section is also designed to touch on several different learning approaches. If you are the kinesthetic type, go straight to the activity and that may be all you'll need to do. If you are more analytical, read the "Going Deeper" that follows each activity. If you are on the practical end of things, you may want to begin with the basic technique. However you begin, follow your intuition and enjoy!

I hope this section will heighten your experience of EmoTrance and give you ideas and ways to heal and nurture your energy system in life.

Add a Few EmoTrance Activities to Your Day

I suggest that the very first additions to your day be the EmoTrance activities of "Greeting the Day" and "Greeting the Night".

Greeting the Day

Step outside as soon as you have risen or simply open a window.

- Breathe in deeply.
- Say, "Day, I greet you."

- Allow this day to come to you, to bring you its totally unique properties.
- State your intention, "I receive this unique energy into all my systems."
- Pay attention to any physical responses you might have to this experience.
- Check for any emotions or stuck energy.
- Place your hand there and soften the sensation.
- Breathe.
- Soften and flow until the energy runs clearly.
- Check again for any sensations of pressure, discomfort, nervousness, or of rejecting this day, etc.
- Soften and flow until the energy runs smoothly.
- Come back to your breath.
- One more time, re-state the words, "Day, I greet you."
- Remain still and say, "Thank you, Day, for your unique lessons."
- Step back inside and into your ordinary life.

Greeting the Night

- When the night sky is present, step outside.
- Take a moment to look around, to get into rapport with the night and become a little more still and a little more observant.
- Breathe.
- Say, "Night, I greet you."
- Check yourself for any physiological sensations, emotions, or "stuck" energy that might have accumulated during the day.
- Soften and flow. Allow the night to take away what is no longer needed, drawing it up into its endless self.

- Say, "Night I greet you."
- Give a sincere, "Thank you" for the day's journey, all its lessons and to the night for its assistance in clearing away energies into its vast abundance.
- Be still.
- Come back to your breath.
- Return to your normal activities.

A Thought

Each day has its own unique properties and gifts. "Greeting the Day" and "Greeting the Night" allow you to connect on a universal plane, reminding you that you are not alone before continuing on with your life. These exercises take just a few moments of your time each day but in energetic terms they are truly profound and help to balance, soothe, heal, and energize.

Basic Technique

These activities are best done outside, no matter whether the day is rainy or sunny, hot or cold, windy or still. The elements add to the distinctiveness of that day. No two days are ever quite the same and each one will hold its own unique qualities that will be different from tomorrow and already has its own place in comparison to yesterday.

If you are unable to get outside, open a window. With the day or night energies swirling in around you, these activities can adjust and work quite well.

Digging Deeper

I love stepping outside to greet the night. Here I give thanks for the day and all the lessons it brought to me. Here I welcome the night and a time to rest and reflect. Sometimes I stand outside with my arms raised to the heavens and other times I just stand. I soften and flow and, at times, I am filled with radiant energy. Here under the sky, I search for symptoms of *Energioso Stuckitis* and use the EmoTrance process to flow energy through those areas.

If you are having any difficulty clearing energies, merely your intention to move these energies may do so. Over time you will get better with this activity until simply the action of going outside will begin the process and may even complete it as well! If you do not feel that all the energy is cleared, continue on in love and gratitude for the time spent knowing that each time you do this you are healing.

For the night activity, look especially for any *Energioso Stuckitis* that might have accumulated during the day and soften it. Silvia Hartmann states that, "...in your dealings with 'The Hard', allow the night to take away whatever is no longer needed, drawing all this up and into its endless self. You will notice that with even two or three repetitions, your ability to channel energy from the day and night increases dramatically as your systems and their pathways are becoming clearer and more efficient."

Above all, remember to give a sincere, "Thank You," to the night for its assistance and its lessons before you return to your evening routine.

When you begin these activities, you might find that you strongly "take from the day" and "release to the night". But as time goes by, you may find that what is happening is a true circular exchange with both the day and the night. Each have their own unique lessons and energies to give as well as assisting you in taking what is no longer needed.

It is a beautiful and very moving exercise that benefits you in many more ways than you might suspect. Do the exercise for a week and you will begin to know just how much support and sustenance there is for you simply by virtue of being there.

EmoTrance Activities for Flowing Energy

Adding just a few simple activities to your life will help energy to flow into, through, and out of your system.

Drawing in Energies

A Thought

There are energies all around us. Being able to draw in these energies through our energy system can sustain, nourish, and revive the energy system at any given time.

Basic Technique

You can choose to draw energy in from just about anything in your environment such as water, food, air...anything. If you can take a walk in nature and find a tree or plant to draw energy from, it can be a good way to begin your experience.

- Become aware of the object or thing you will be using and place it in front of you.
- Breathe.
- Where do you feel this in your body?
- Where else do you feel it in your body? Soften and flow.
- Where does the energy want to go? Soften and flow.
- Continue until you reach the energized end state.
- Come back to your breath.

Digging Deeper

Taking in the tremendous amount of energy from the environment is one way to nurture your body. This activity is also a very good way to practice EmoTrance and to heighten your awareness of the energies around you and how they can course through your energy system at any given time.

You will be surprised as you go along how much energy is available to you that was not there until you learned EmoTrance. This is a tremendous gift of this modality.

Have a Nice Day

A Thought

Every day we have phrases we use to those around us when we say hello, such as, "Thank you," and "Have a nice day." Seasonally there are common phrases we express to each other as well, such as, "Merry Christmas," or "Happy Hanukah." There is so much energy in the expression of words, especially when they come in the form of good wishes from another person or when you are the giver of the kind words.

What you may not know is that these words, in and of themselves, hold energy. Every thought you have is refined energy. Knowing this and using EmoTrance can give more energy to the words, adding to their vibration in you or to the receiver. These phrases can nourish you and fill you with energy or be a gift to another as you flow them with energy. (If you flow kind words to another and they are not well received, not to worry, that person probably has a shield.)

Basic Technique

Pay attention to others around you. As you move along in your day someone may say to you, "Thank you," "Have a nice day," "Merry Christmas," or many other kinds of words depending on the circumstances. EmoTrance the phrases as they are expressed to you. When you are expressing good wishes, soften as you breathe in and flow as you speak the words with the out breath.

- Have a nice day.
- Where do you feel that in your body?
- Show yourself with your hands.
- Place all your attention there.
- Soften and flow.
- Repeat until you achieve *Even Flow*.

You are giving a greeting to another. Any expression will work, so soften and as you flow, say to the individual, " Good morning," or any greeting.

- Think about the words you are about to say.
- Where do you feel them in your body?

- Place your full attention there.
- Breathe in the word and say, "soften," and think of the word.
- Breathe out and think, "flow," as you say, "Have a nice day," to that individual.
- Take a note of what you are experiencing in your body.

Digging Deeper

Giving and receiving are the gifts life offers. Often I think we are here as human beings for the sole purpose of practicing how to give and receive in the full continuum of life.

Using EmoTrance to flow the words of another helps to heighten the energy nutrition in that moment and lets the words of another flow through your energy system.

Using EmoTrance to flow your own words brings a great gift of energy to the receiver that probably will be a surprise to their energy system. Do not worry if it goes unnoticed or if there is no response; your gift will continue to flow with the energy of life.

With practice you will find you are able to send energy out in a stronger way than you thought possible.

EmoTrance Activities to Manage Stress

Both insults and compliments can cause energy to become stuck in your system. These simple activities will get it flowing.

Insults

(also found in the EmoTrance Examples with the Sixth Grade)

A Thought

The purpose of the insults activity is to empower you with the ability to flow hurtful words through your energy system without them creating a blockage and back flow of energy over time. In fact, it will free you of any affect a word or words may have had on you in the past. This is such a powerful activity, giving you back control of your emotions instead of your emotions controlling you.

Basic Technique

Find a partner to help you with this. The difficult part about this activity is that the individual you select often does not want to participate because they do not want to insult you. But casting insults at each other is the very thing that will free you both from their ability to hurt you. It is important when doing this activity that you finish at the point of *Even Flow* and reach the energized end state which often appears in the form of laughter.

Your partner asks what insult you would like said to you.
- Example: You say, "You are ugly."
- Partner repeats, "You are ugly!"
- Then partner states, "Where do you feel that in your body?"
- Place your hands there and give it your full attention.
- Soften and flow.
- When you are done, ask the partner to repeat the insult.
- Use the EmoTrance Process until your partner states the insult and you find yourself freely flowing the energy. You may find yourself laughing or having feelings of light-heartedness.
- Repeat and give your partner an opportunity to experience this activity.
- If time is available, find another insult.

Digging Deeper

Often in life you may try to control what is happening by eliminating whatever is wrong or offending you. This makes sense right? Yet, at times, you find what you avoid or try and get rid of can be worse if it returns.

Abraham Hicks states, "You simply cannot get to where you want to be by controlling or eliminating the unwanted." Although you cannot control things you do not want, you can flow them through your energy system with EmoTrance until they no longer bother you. In fact, you may find yourself smiling at times!

Eleanor Roosevelt's said, "No one can make you feel inferior without your consent." The same is true for insults. Let me paraphrase that quote a little, "No one can hurt you with words without your consent." What would your consent be then? Consent would represent the judgment you give the word you consider an insult as "bad" or "insulting" or "hurtful".

From the EmoTrance perspective, the emotion you feel behind the word or the energy you give a word is exactly that—it's only energy!

Compliments

A Thought

Did you know that you are amazing? You have challenged yourself to learn a new skill to enhance your ability to experience life to the fullest.

You are amazing!

How do you feel when you hear yourself being praised? Do you embrace the compliment or shy away from it. Some people have a hard time accepting compliments and praise.

There are two ways to use EmoTrance. You can flow energy when you are insulted and when you are praised.

EmoTrance does not prevent bad things from happening, but it does give you a tool to make it through whatever happens along your life's journey. Not only does it help you make it through, but it helps you to rediscover the joy at the other end of the energy that becomes stuck because of what was said.

Basic Technique

This technique is similar to the insults activity. Find a partner and a quiet place to have fun complimenting each other. Do not analyze why a compliment may be uncomfortable. Simply bringing up the energy is often enough to flow it. It is important to give the compliment the emotional energy of admiration that comes with it. This will assist in bringing up any stuck energy in your partner that may need to be moved.

You can also practice this activity by yourself in front of a mirror by giving yourself compliments. Even when you are alone, this can be transforming

- Greet your partner or yourself in a mirror.
- Tell your partner what compliment you may have trouble receiving.
- An example, you can begin with, "You are an amazing person!"
- Your partner compliments you.
- EmoTrance the energy in your body.
- Have your partner tell you again.
- Repeat until you reach the energized end state.

Digging Deeper

A true compliment holds a positive "voice" or a higher vibrational energy and a negative compliment holds a "negative" voice or a lower vibrational energy. It is often hard to handle a higher vibrational energy, like a compliment, if you are in a lower vibrational state.

Lower vibrational energy states are often a part of our daily lives and the lives of those around us. These lower vibrations are created from the stressors of negative self talk or what I would call "a rough day".

When the energy vibration states don't match up, you are not in a receptive place and a compliment will be hard to handle. With the constant onslaught of negativity that may exist in your environment, this activity can begin to activate a higher vibration within you as you learn how to soften and flow the energy that becomes stuck without your knowing it.

A friend of mine calls these inner negative voices or frequencies, "the ladies in the attic". The ladies are the voices of her negative self putting her down because of her weight, her attitude, or her life in general.

When we practiced this activity together, it was hard for my friend to accept a compliment. First the energy was in her head, then it flowed to her chest and it took several EmoTrance attempts until she was laughing and reached an energized end state and felt the wonderful tingle of energy through her.

We practiced the compliment again until it flowed from her chest into her core, but she no longer wanted to flow it. She "liked" the compliment and didn't want to let it go.

I explained to her that all energy needs to flow, whether it is something good like a compliment or difficult to hear like an insult. All energy needs to flow through us and nourish us and not get stuck in us, even if it is a compliment. (It is only energy!)

But my friend doesn't get enough compliments and was having trouble letting the energy go! I encouraged her to soften and flow and the energy in her core eventually went to her back for awhile before clearing.

My friend then experienced the wonderful tingle of energy flow from the energized end state and realized that the flow of energy coursing through her was more powerful than holding on to any compliment.

These two EmoTrance activities, insults and compliments, can be wonderful ways to help you evolve your energy system to receive higher vibrational energies from all around you.

Energy Shower

A Thought

This is a beautiful exercise for relieving stress.

You can stress your body until it can literally start to weigh you down and "depress you". It can feel like the joy is being pressed out of you and the weight of the world is on your shoulders. It is well-known that stress is one of the major causes of depression and many other diseases in our society. The more stress you can release, the less negativity you will experience and the happier you will be.

This exercise uses the innocent energy around you to heal and ease away stress.

Basic Technique

Breath becomes central to relieving stress because shallow breathing is one of the first signs of stress. So breathe! This is a visualization activity and can be done anywhere. It is most effective, though, if you can find a quiet place and can put yourself in a comfortable seated position.

- Relax.
- Breathe deeply and slowly in and out for three breaths.
- Imagine yourself under an energy shower.
- Tiny, microscopic droplets of energy with a temperature perfect for you are raining down on and through you.
- Let this energy trickle through your entire body, refreshing everything, cleansing, healing.
- Especially have it run over an area in your body that feels particularly tight or dense or heavy—this is where you are holding the stress.
- Feel how this lovely rain of energy is softening and melting all the stress.
- Soften and flow. Where does the energy want to go?
- Follow the energy flow as it finds its way out.
- Take note of how your feelings are gradually changing and getting lighter.
- Bring your hands to your shoulders and squeeze your muscles, assisting the tingly release of energy through your body.
- Massage a little more if needed.
- Come back to your breath.
- Breathe gently in and out.

Digging Deeper

With the help of the energy shower, *Energioso Stuckitis* in the body is able to flow through the channels that were designed to carry the energy away. Feeling it flow down or up the channels and out your body brings you the awareness of the ability of the energy system to repair itself simply by the intention you have to let it do so. With that intention, the energy finds its way out of your body, freeing up your energy system to allow *Even Flow* to happen.

With *Even Flow* happening, more of your life will be in "flow".

You can do this at any time, anywhere, and the more you remember to do this, the better you get at instant stress relief, using nothing but the real feelings in your body that tell you where you carry your stress and a little flow of energy. You can also listen to a version of this for free at: http://emotrance. com/the_superfast_emotrance_stress_release_technique.htm

Letting Go of Shields

A Thought

During the EmoTrance process, you may come across a situation or hurt that you do not feel in your body, which may be because of an energetic shield. A shield is designed to protect the energetic body so that it does not get hurt, but it is also depriving you of energy nutrition. Understanding shields is one of the single most fascinating EmoTrance skills that you can explore to make a dramatic change over time in your energy system. Becoming aware of shields and dissolving them is a wonderful tool to have.

Basic Technique

The first part of dissolving shields is identifying one that is a part of your makeup. Find a situation that you either do not feel in your body, something you "don't like", or something to which you feel you have no connection.

For instance, you find a situation you would prefer to keep at "arm's length" or something you have rejected. It could be a computer, a bill, a spider, a vegetable or maybe a skill you do not think you have, to name a few ideas.

The technique involves first imagining a shield around you protecting you from what you want to avoid. The next part of the technique will gradually bring you to dissolving the shield and allowing more energy into your energy system.

- Identify a person or situation that has hurt you that you don't feel in your body or look at a picture or something written to "evoke the energy" for you.

- Visualize an energetic shield around you protecting you from that situation.
- Where is the shield? Show me with your hands.
- Make a small pinhole in the shield.
- Allow a small stream of energy to flow through the pinhole into you. A stream small enough to give you just a "taste" of that energy.
- Where do you feel that in your body?
- Soften and flow.
- Trace the channels of incoming energy from where it enters in, through, and finally out.
- Repeat as needed.
- Please Note: When working with pathways or channels that lie behind a shield, be advised that these pathways might not have been used in a long time and they may well be in an underdeveloped state. It is important to proceed *very gently* in the next stages.
- If you continue to have trouble, consult a Credentialed EmoTrance Practitioner or seek qualified advice from other professionals.
- For more information, go to www.EmoTrance.com.

Digging Deeper

The single most effective EmoTrance technique that has changed my life is learning how to let go of energetic shields. I did not even know they existed before I studied EmoTrance.

My shields had been constructed to protect me and my energy body from further hurt because of situations that I found difficult or painful from childhood to adulthood. Because I had no control over them and lacked awareness of their presence, I had many painful situations in my life that kept repeating themselves.

I found I had a shield to just about everything—people, friends, family, learning—you name it. As I discovered these shields and learned to let them go, I found myself absorbing the energies of life and getting nurtured by a multitude of energies around me. I was finally on a diet of easy-to-receive energy. I had been unaware I was starving for energy.

Letting go of shields has taught me how to love to the fullest for almost any person, place or thing, because "love has no shields". I found that once my shields to others were dissolved, I was able to fully absorb the energy of another person.

As I absorbed the energy of others in my presence, it became apparent to me through words and actions that others felt "accepted" by me and comfortable in my presence.

Another noticeable occurrence for me was that if I was absorbing the energy of another person, I could not judge her or him at the same time. That lack of judgment immediately allowed others to feel more accepted by me.

What greater way to love and accept another than to say to them in a subconscious way (by flowing their energy),"You nourish me. Your very being nourishes me and is worthy of passing through my energy system." This connection is a combination of receiving, letting go, and allowing the flow of energy to come in. It is ultimately a sense of "oneness".

I found that love is letting go of shields—shields of fear, prejudice, judgment and condemnation. In this shieldless state, I have found a new way of simply being me.

Using Your Healing Hands

A Thought

If you have been experiencing a great deal of stress in your life, you may have examined a variety of stress-relieving modalities. You probably never considered one of the best tools you have are your own hands.

Emotions are the feedback we get from our energy body giving us direction in life. EmoTrance theorizes that, like your physical body, you have an energy body made up of energy arms, feet, legs and hands.

Your hands of energy are "healing hands". They are usually in the same place as your physical hands, but not awakened to healing until you consciously activate them by giving them the intention to heal. Once your healing hands are activated, they can touch your body and ease away stress, emotional discomfort, or other energetic injuries that are felt as energy blockages.

Look at your hands. Focus on the right hand for a few seconds. Now give your full attention to your left hand. Do you feel more energy in one hand than you do in the other? Very often that is the case and the hand with the stronger energy sensation is your giving hand and the hand with less is the receiving hand. This represents the importance of giving and receiving in our lives.

Thus, your hands have an incredible power to heal, starting with you! This activity will help you move away from thinking about the problem to concentrating on where that problem lives in your body and using your hands to assist in flowing it out of your body the EmoTrance way.

This exercise is different from earlier EmoTrance activities that used your thought intention to flow energy. In this exercise, you surrender the healing process to the incredible ability inherent in your hands. How does this take place? Again, this happens with your intention to create a healing process through your hands, as well as the natural capability that your hands have to do so.

Basic Technique

Again, find a quiet place to enjoy this activity and sit in a comfortable position. Before you being this activity, practice the following energy awareness method: clap your hands and then rub them together. Stop and hold them out in front of you. Do you feel the tingling of energy in your hands? Hold your hands so that they face each other without touching. Do you feel the ball of energy between your hands? Oscillate your hands back and forth to feel this energy. Do not let your hands touch!

This is the energy of your healing hands that you will use for this activity. This activity will involve you thinking about a problem, finding where it lives in your body and placing your hands there to warm it, before stroking, softening, and flowing it away.

- Breathe.
- Clap your hands together.
- Vigorously rub your hands together.
- Draw them apart. Become aware of the tingly energy.
- Identify the problem.
- Where does it live in your body?
- Look at your hands and set the intention that they can heal and smooth away the energy block in your body.
- Hold your hands above the area of blockage.
- Feel the warmth of your hands passing to the body, dissolving the blockage.
- Smooth away the blockage with your hands.
- Say, "Soften and flow."
- Continue the light massaging, caressing motions with your hands as you guide the energy out of your body.
- Say, "Soften and flow," as a mantra as you follow the energy out.
- Take feedback from the sensations and stay focused on healing.
- Repeat as needed.
- Breathe.
- Look at your hands and say "Thank you, thank you, thank you."
- Bring your hands together to end the exercise.

Digging Deeper

As we turn to the hands, a higher sense of spirit becomes present. We have a physical body and an energy body. Our energy body has energy arms, hands, legs, feet, head, eyes, etc. Our healing hands reveal to us how powerful they can be, when the physical and energy bodies work as one.

Healing Hands and a Partner

A Thought

There is nothing like healing hands to massage away stress. Healing hands massage applies EmoTrance to healing touch when working with a partner. But where do you begin when you have little experience with massaging another? That is easy when it comes to EmoTrance!

Simply ask, "If these hands could heal, where would you want them to go?"

Basic Technique

Your partner can be sitting in a chair or lying on a comfortable supportive surface. Although this can be done over clothing, it is more efficacious if you can put your hands directly on the skin. Using a lotion or massage oil can decrease the friction of the skin and add to the comfort of your hands on the person's body.

When your hands are on an area of stress or discomfort, before following the EmoTrance sequence, take a SUE level (as shown in Figure 2, page 22).

Why is it important to take a SUE measurement? The SUE scale allows your partner to see how much of the pain is dissipating. The partner will be amazed at how much discomfort can be released by simply softening and flowing.

- Make sure your partner is comfortable.
- Ask your partner, "If these hands could heal, where would you want them to go?" (Remember to always ask permission before touching anyone.)
- Place your hands on that area and leave them there for three seconds.
- Ask your partner, "On a scale of 1 to 10, with 1 being no stress to 10 being maximum stress, how much stress do you feel in this area?"
- After the response, instruct your partner to soften and flow.

- Ask your partner, "Where does the stress energy want to go?"
- Follow the cues of your partner and follow the flow of the energy with your hands.
- Repeat the process until the energy is flowing freely.

Movement and EmoTrance

Physical movement can help to get energy moving. Don't underestimate the power of movement.

The Stretch

A Thought

Physical movement is a key factor in flowing energy. The beauty of stretching is that it pulls energy into the body. Stretching can be restorative in times of stress.

Basic Technique

You can also perform this technique with any stretches that you know.

Dress comfortably if possible, but it is not necessary. The main objective of this technique is to get a joint or part of the body to an extended, comfortable length, holding, and then slowly releasing it back to the starting position. This can be done while lying down in bed, sitting in a chair, or standing. For this exercise, we will be stretching in a standing position.

A key to this technique is to do it slowly and, when the stretch is released, to feel the tingle of energy flowing into and through your body.

- Stand with your feet hip width apart, hands at your sides.
- As you take a deep breath, reach your right arm as high as you can, as though you are trying to touch the ceiling.
- Hold.
- Slowly bring the arm back to your side. Release your breath.
- Experience the flow of energy in you.

- Is it tingly? Is it warm? Where is the energy going?
- Repeat with your left arm.
- Relax and come back to your breath.
- Repeat as needed using your favorite stretches.

Digging Deeper

As with many facets of life, when stress is heightened and life is moving too quickly, there tends to be a disconnect between the physical body and the energy body.

Taking time to stretch and experience the flow of energy entering and moving through your body is empowering. Starting your day with a routine stretch and ending the day with a few stretches helps energy flow to where it is needed for your life's journey.

Energy Dancing

A Thought

What if you danced every day from this day forward? Does that sound like a joy-filled life?

I had a friend who told me she could not dance. Energy dancing proved her wrong.

Energy dancing invites you to use natural, gentle movements to unlock your energy system and increase energy flow through your whole body while decreasing stress and tension.

Moving your body to the vibration of music can be cleansing and energizing on many levels. Give this activity a try to your favorite song or there are excellent CDs from www. Dragonrising.com to enhance your intuitive energy dancing abilities that are designed to help you dance through life.

Basic Technique

Find de-stressing music with a good strong beat along with an empowering rhythm that will assist you in moving and letting the energy flow. If you are in a situation where there is no music available, you can make music by tapping your feet or clapping your hands and singing or humming.

- Turn on your music source.
- Stand in a comfortable position.
- Where do you feel the most stress in your body?
- Show yourself with your hands.
- Now start to move and sway a little with the beat of the music and let your spine find the right movements to help flow more energy to that place of stress.
- Move your hips and your legs to help improve the energy flow. Pay attention to how the movement is helping with the energy flow through your body and how that feels.
- Move your feet, toes, and knees to help with the energy flow.
- Now, start moving your head, neck and shoulders, your arms, your fingers, your face, your eyebrows, your eyes, your mouth and tongue, even your nose until all of you is dancing, all of you is helping you find that place where you feel your stress the most.
- Breathe deeply and enjoy yourself as you get into the music and the feel of the energy in your body as it flows faster and faster and you are feeling more sparkly, electric, and alive.
- When the music ends, jump up and give yourself a round of applause. You just had your first experience of Energy Dancing!

Digging Deeper

Life is one big dance. Energy is flowing in nature, in those around us, in yourself and in your cells, whether you are physically moving or not. Our very breath is a dance of nature. When stressors become overwhelming for our body, the first area to clamp down is our breath. This will affect everything because it carries the oxygen needed to sustain life.

So dance. When you are at home, set a timer to remind you to dance regularly and put on a three minute song and enjoy the movement of energy, the movement of life through you.

Jogging

A Thought

Whenever you have sustained movement over a period of time—by jogging, riding a bike, aerobic exercise, etc.—stress may be present in muscles other than those in constant use. This activity brings EmoTrance into the exercise activity to provide a more relaxed and enjoyable work out!

Basic Technique

For this example, I will use jogging, but the technique can also be performed while walking or performing any aerobic activity. While jogging, focus on your body, scanning for unnecessary muscle tension.

- Place your attention on the muscles of your face and eyes.
- Say, "Soften and flow."
- Give gentle attention to the release of energy flow from your muscles of your eyes.
- Give gentle attention to the release of energy flow from your muscles of your face.
- Repeat.
- Move to your shoulders.
- Place your attention on your shoulder muscles and say, "Soften and flow."
- Give gentle attention to the release of energy flow from these muscles.
- Repeat as needed.

Digging Deeper

Jogging is an activity I have enjoyed over the years. It was not until I brought the technique of EmoTrance into my jogging activity that I recognized how much tension I was holding in my eyes, my face, and shoulder muscles while I exercised. Once I released this tension, I gained an increased awareness of my surroundings and have a more relaxed and enjoyable jogging experience!

Reflection Tools to Bring Healing Moments

These techniques will help you to awaken your inner healer.

Heart Healing

A Thought

The center of our energy body is the energy heart. It is the ruler on how we experience life, what we think, and what we do. All emotions are "cries from the heart" whether they are of love, joy and ecstasy, or fear, sorrow, and pain. Our heart needs special attention to radiate healing to our bodies.

Basic Technique

This can be done anywhere. If you are in a crowded place and are self-conscious about placing your hands on your heart, visualize your energy hands being placed over your heart. This allows your own energy system, which knows best what to do, to help restore the *Even Flow*.

- Put yourself into a comfortable position.
- Take a deep breath in and out.
- Close your eyes and turn an inward focus on your heart.
- Place your healing hands over your heart.
- Recite this poem:

    I put my healing hands
    On my heart of energy.
    To heal what once was broken
    To make right what once went wrong.
    To soften and flow,
    To restore the *Even Flow*
    So that my heart of energy
    Can once again
    Shine like the sun.

- Stay still until you are ready to come back to ordinary awareness.

Digging Deeper

By focusing on healing your heart, you awaken an incredible gift that lies within you. I like to call it "the inner healer". You have the power to heal what lies within you. Why would it be otherwise? Is anyone else in your body?

Today's advertising thrives on financial gain through informing others that without this "drug" or this "weight-loss system", etc. (which they are positive will work for you), you cannot heal the issues with which you may be confronted.

I ask you, "Are *they* in your body? Do *they* really know what you are experiencing? Do *they* hear the voice of your heart?"

Learning to follow your heart, learning to heal your heart, is a tremendous empowering gift you can give yourself. You will journey through a process of self-discovery in ways you cannot imagine because it is *your* life, *your* journey, and *your* heart, and *no one else's.*

The beauty of EmoTrance is that you are unique and the absolute guide to your own energy system. EmoTrance Practitioners know this and will help you to use your energy system to heal yourself.

Beginning with Heart Healing and practicing this regularly, you can start to embrace the You that you have always wanted to be and to get to know yourself again.

Attitude of Gratitude

A Thought

Cultivating gratitude and appreciation is one of the easier paths to developing a deeper sense of emotional well-being. Living in gratitude heightens the *Even Flow* of your energy system.

There are many ways to cultivate gratitude. Using EmoTrance to flow gratitude, especially at the beginning of the day, often results in more positive experiences throughout the day. You will notice you have less of a tendency to focus on negative or stressful events when gratitude is at the forefront of your day. Feelings of "lack" tend to melt away and you will find yourself having a greater appreciation for the people and things in your life.

When creating more abundance in your life, gratitude and appreciation are considered key areas to develop.

Basic Technique

If you like to journal, keeping a gratitude journal is a wonderful way to heighten this EmoTrance experience. Take a moment to reflect on what you are grateful for and write it down. Even if you do this for only two minutes a day, it will have a cumulative effect and you will find yourself living more and more in the flow. After you write down or think about what you are grateful for, EmoTrance each one and allow it to flow freely through your body.

- Connect with your breath.
- State out loud something that you are grateful for.
- Use the EmoTrance process until you reach *Even Flow*.
- Come back to your breath.
- Feel the energy of gratitude coursing through your system.
- Repeat.

Digging Deeper

This is a wonderful EmoTrance activity for me that often brings tears of gratefulness to my eyes. I do this activity in the morning after I greet the day and, on occasion, under the night sky or when resting in bed after I finished greeting the night. I pick something I am grateful for and follow the EmoTrance process. For example, I am so grateful for my husband, Kevin. Where do I feel this in my body? My heart. I soften and flow until I achieve *Even Flow*". It is a beautiful way to stay in vibration with all that I have to be grateful for.

I will go on to flow other things for which I am grateful—I am grateful for this day, water, food, my computer, my eyes, my children...and the list goes on. One cannot help but be in a state of flow and joy following this activity.

Why focus on this activity? Studies show that cultivating a sense of gratitude can help you maintain a more positive emotional focus in daily life. It also shows that gratitude naturally brings greater emotional well-being and a feeling of abundance. Next to love, gratitude is known to promote one of the highest vibrations of the universe. Many personal development speakers point to gratitude as the main avenue towards wealth development.

Practicing Self-Compassion

A Thought

How kind are you to yourself? I recently read a study on self-compassion by Dr. Kristin Neff from the University of Texas. The study pointed out that people who are compassionate and supportive of others are often the ones who have more issues with anxiety and depression. Are you as compassionate to yourself as you are to your friends when things go wrong? Or, do you berate yourself for not doing things right? People who are self-compassionate turn out to be happier and more optimistic. Taking care of yourself and treating yourself gently when things go wrong, may be a critical first step needed to reduce stress in your life.

Basic Technique

You need to create opportunities to practice self compassion on a regular basis. First, listen to how you treat your friends when things go wrong in their lives. Find your common phrases. For example:

- "Not to worry, it will be just fine."
- "It was just accident; it could happen to anyone!"
- "It may not have turned out the way you planned, but you gave it your best shot, you should be proud of yourself!"

Once you find these main phrases, place yourself in the same situations and use these compassionate phrases to practice treating yourself more kindly.

Picture a time when you "messed up" or did something that made you feel bad about yourself. Choose a self-compassionate phrase (comfort phrase) and state it out loud. For example:

- "Not to worry, it will be just fine."
- Where do you feel that in your body?
- Show yourself with your hands.
- Say, "Soften and flow."
- Breathe deeply.
- As you exhale, say the comfort phrase and feel the exhale slowly caressing you.
- Come back to your breath.
- Repeat as needed.

This exercise is great to try while looking in a mirror.

Digging Deeper:

Being "hard" on yourself has been viewed in our society as a way to get ourselves in shape. Being kind to ourselves has been looked on as self-indulgent, soft, or weak. Yet, this is the very step we need to take to a happier, more vibrant life.

When traveling in an airplane, the safety instructions tell you that if the plane is loosing altitude to first put on your oxygen mask before assisting a child or another passenger. This makes sense. What good are you if you do not take care of yourself first? This is the same with compassion. What can you truly give to another if you do not take care of yourself first? Giving out the oxygen of love to our own spirits through the act of self-compassion can prevent the blockages often caused by negative self-talk. Using EmoTrance to release your inner critique may be the next step to a healthier you.

For more information go to www.self-compassion.org.

Conclusion

I hope the exercises in Section II have helped you to improve your ability and understanding of how to flow energy with the technique of EmoTrance.

Using EmoTrance can also help you to become emotionally fit. I first became aware of the concept of emotional fitness in an article by Sandra Hillawi on her website, passionforhealth.com. She drew a comparison between the importance of physical fitness and emotional fitness. Because I am a physical therapist as well as an EmoTrance Practitioner, I believe this anology is very important.

In our society, great emphasis is placed on physical fitness to an extent that a key to overall fitness—emotional well-being—is often left out. Emotional fitness may be the very thing that drives us towards striving to be physically fit and vice versa. So, although our society has an emphasis on physical fitness, without emotional fitness is true physical fitness possible?

Let us look at physical fitness in preparation for playing a sport. Before you begin you will need warm up activities, followed by stretching, and then it is game time. Following the game, cool down times are needed, plus time for overall recovery.

You can find your emotional fitness warm up activities in "Greeting the Day", game time exercises in the stress relieving activities, and cool down in "Greeting the Night". The game of life is to be played full out and having the tool of EmoTrance can assist you in living an emotionally fit life.

Our quest for emotional fitness through the EmoTrance process can help you devise a way to use these tools to assist you in handling the ups and downs you encounter as you go on to live a life of grace and ease.

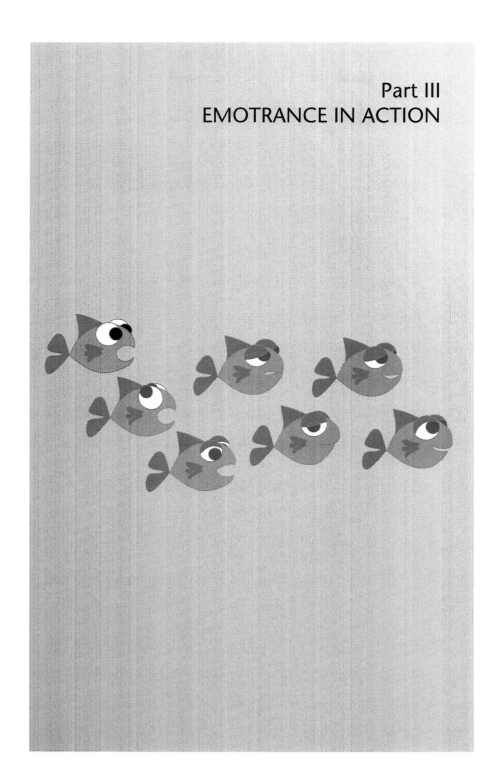

Part III
EMOTRANCE IN ACTION

Case Histories

This last section includes four examples of EmoTrance in action. Two of the examples were private, one-on-one sessions where the client gave me permission to tape the session to share with you. The first dealt with a fear of flying and the other with a gentleman who is a highly successful surgeon whose stress involved internalized anger.

The third and fourth sessions were chosen because they explored the EmoTrance process in a group situation. The third session involved a sixth-grade class to help them reduce math testing anxiety and the fourth a group of nurses at a social gathering where a discussion about the need for stress management techniques flowed (of course) right into an EmoTrance conversation!

These four situations have been chosen to guide you in a greater understanding of the process of EmoTrance and I hope they will help you in explaining EmoTrance to another person, if needed.

Following each session there will be an opportunity for you to reflect more fully on each session and apply it to your own experience and healing. There are also activities to help you get in tune with the "flow" of

"Your intention is not meant to direct the energy flow through your body, but to follow the sensations in order to discover where this flow naturally wants to go and to assist if there are any problems with the natural pathways."

energies moving within you, and to help you become more sensitive and more aware of their movement.

I have worked with a variety of clients in numerous different situations. In response to feeling the stuck energy move and change locations as it was dissipating, many of my clients often state after an EmoTrance session that, "I never knew it (the energy) could do that (move the energy out)! All this time I had this stuck energy and all I had to do was ask it to leave?"

You may see some of that reflected here.

An EmoTrance Experience: Flight Anxiety

In this session, the key EmoTrance steps that were described in Figure 1, page 22, are highlighted. I took time to emphasize certain concepts to assist the client in a greater understanding of EmoTrance. The client also asked a few questions about the healing process. These were left in because they may answer questions you have and assist you in further understanding your healing process and transformations.

Margaret, a lovely 46-year-old woman, came to me for problems with anxiety brought on by a fear of flying. Margaret was going to be flying in an airplane with her family on a vacation to the Caribbean Islands and didn't know how she was going to manage her flight anxiety.

Fear of turbulence, along with the excruciating, painful thought of "anticipating the sudden stop if the plane should suddenly take a nosedive to earth", lingered in her mind. She had used EFT (emotional freedom technique) in the past which helped somewhat, but her problem persisted.

As we sat together, I spoke to her about EmoTrance and she quickly responded that she had never heard of it, but was willing to try anything.

I asked her, "When I say the word "plane", where do you feel that in your body?"

"Oh, in my stomach," she responded.

"Show me with your hands," I said.

She took her hands and placed them on the exact location. There was no doubt where the injury to her energy system was manifesting itself.

I asked her, "Where else do you feel the word 'plane' in your body?"

At first she responded, "Nowhere," but then she stopped and thought for a moment before replying, "Wait a minute, I also feel it here in my heart." She had naturally moved one hand to the location.

To empower her further, I said, "Think about where your hands are. You feel discomfort under your hands? (She nodded yes.) That is the exact location of the damage to your energy system. The emotions you are experiencing in the form of anxiety right now are cries of pain from your energy system."

"I have to say," she responded, "The tension there really keeps me from functioning and doing what I need to do around the house. But I have ignored it in the past. I pushed it aside, saying, 'be tough and move on,' because I told myself nothing was wrong with me. I've told myself, 'It's all in my head!' (She laughed as she looked at where her hands where). But, I guess that's not true.

"So, how would this then be different from a physical problem?" she asked reflectively relaxing her hands into her lap.

"A physical problem or pain that you are having in your knee or a pain resulting from something such as a broken bone, would tell you the status of what is happening to your skeletal system and that the bone is in need of repair. You go to the doctor who orders an x-ray and, sure enough, it is broken. The pain you are having is verified on x-ray." Margaret nodded attentively as I continued the explanation:

"With emotional pain, like you are having now, you can feel exactly where it is, you can feel how intense it is, possibly know how long you have had it, and you may even have felt something was seriously wrong with that spot. Yet, if you went to the doctor and received an x-ray, cat scan, or MRI of that exact location, the report would most likely tell you that nothing is wrong. The doctor would not be able to explain why you have pain there." Margaret showed agreement in her facial expression.

"Today we know that, as EmoTrance creator Silvia Hartmann stated, 'all emotions are cries of joy or pain from your energy system.' You are experiencing a cry of pain from your energy system when you have anxiety, whether it is a result of a fear of flying or anything else."

"Well, how do I get it to leave?"

"It may sound simplistic, but your intention to do so by using EmoTrance. EmoTrance is one way. There are other techniques out there today as well."

"So, you are not going to do anything to me, I am going to do it myself?" Margaret asked with a quizzical look on her face.

"Yes," I replied. "and I'll guide you through it! Remember, the bone problem? When the doctor sets the broken bone, she or he does not really heal the injured person. The doctor simply puts the bone in a better position so that the person's body could do best what it already knows how to do, and that is to heal itself!

"It is the same for a damaged energy system. Put it in a position to heal and it will do what it does best—heal—or in the case of energy, it will flow.

"There is a popular EmoTrance motto that says that the energy system, when given the opportunity, can 'make right what once went wrong!' Your body does this quite well and so does your energy body which makes up your energy system. Put your energy body in a position to heal and it will do so. EmoTrance is a modality which assists in doing just that, putting the energy body in a position to heal so that it can clear away the blocked energy that is causing your pain.

"Now, let's go back to your original problem. When I say the word 'plane', where do you feel that in your body?" I asked. "Show me with your hands."

She placed her hands on her abdomen.

"Where else in your body do you feel it?" I asked.

"I feel it in my heart also", she replied as she moved one hand to her heart.

"How does it feel?" (she shrugged in uncertainty), "Is it hard as ice or murky, for example?" I added.

"It's hard like a rock in my stomach and murky in my heart," she responded.

"Ask the energy there to soften, to soften and flow." I paused before asking, "Where does the energy want to go?"

"Out," she said. "Out through my throat and now to a spot right here." She pointed to a place right behind her chin. "It seems to be stuck there."

"How does that energy feel?" I asked.

"It's odd because it's tingly," she said.

"Can you get that area to soften and flow? Where does the energy want to go?"

"It's just going out, it's better now. It's leaving."

"Keep going," I encouraged her. "Take your time, soften and flow, keep the energy moving out." I waited patiently, giving Margaret time to experience and process the movement of energy within her. Again I repeated gently several times as needed, "Soften and flow, keep going, good job, you are doing great."

A blossoming look of delight came to her face, "Wow, I felt a rush of energy go through me! I feel like I can clean my whole house. Not that I want to," she laughed jokingly.

"What you are describing is the energized end state. You began with anxiety and through the EmoTrance process, the energy flowed and was transformed to joy. I can tell just by looking at your face! Good work!"

"Yes, it's giving me goose bumps," she said.

"So when I say 'plane', where do you feel that in your body?" I asked.

"Wow! I don't feel it right now," she exclaimed, "But I am sure I will feel it later when the time gets closer to getting on a plane again!"

"Like everything in life, practice is a key ingredient to perfecting any skill. It's the same with the modality of EmoTrance. When you make EmoTrance a regular practice in your life, flowing energy will become second nature to you."

"I look forward to that happening!" she replied with some relief.

Time to Pause

Relieving Anxiety

- Think of a time when you have felt anxious.
- How does this feeling differ from physical pain you have experienced in the past or are currently experiencing now?
- Pause
- Margaret said that when dealing with emotional pain, she had to "be tough and move on" and that it was "all in her head". Yet, the damage to the energy system was located in her abdomen and heart regions.

- Have you embraced this emotional pain with the same consideration you would give physical pain or have you tried to push it away?
- Pause
- The body can heal itself. It knows what to do. This is the same for a damaged energy system. Put it in a position to heal and it will do what it does best—heal, or in the case of energy, it will flow. EmoTrance can help to heal the energy body.
- What is your opinion about the energy system needing to be put into an optimal position to heal—that it *can* heal?
- Pause
- Again, try to recall a time when you felt anxious or angry and try to follow the EmoTrance guide in Figure 1. Relax, turn your attention within, and be attentive to the gentle energies within you. For this first time, just observe what is happening within.
- How did the tool work for you? Were you able to feel the energy move?
- Pause

Here is a thought to remember: Your intention is not meant to direct the energy flow through your body, but to "...follow the sensations in order to discover where this flow naturally wants to go and to assist if there are any problems with the natural pathways." (EmoTrance Practitioner Course, S. Hartmann)

Everything is Energy

Time to Pause

Experiencing Finer Energy and Learning to Follow with Intention

- You can do this on your own or with a partner.
- Touch yourself or have your partner lightly touch you with a fingertip on the arm or some other part of the body.

- Follow the sensations of the touch. Pay close attention to where and how far the sensations travel.
- Stay with that for a few moments.
- Now, tap or lightly massage the area.
- As you experience the tap or massage, follow with conscious awareness of the sensations as they discover a pathway all the way through your body and an exit point where this energy naturally leaves your physical systems.
- Encourage flow if there are any areas which hurt and block the flow, or where it dissipates, with the healing intention of soften and flow.
- Notice if you find any blockages to the flow of energy along the way.
- Repeat until you can feel the energy flow instantly and smoothly all the way through and out.
- When it flows smoothly and swiftly, tap your arm or body some more until you get a rushing, tingling sensation that is beyond merely being pleasant but is actually highly charged and delightful.
- Pause
- Did you experience the energy flow?
- The last step of this activity may take time. Simply be aware of the river of energy flowing through you.

If this is your first attempt at following the energy of a light touch, you may not feel the energy flow. When doing this with my husband, he was not able to feel the energy flow of light touch. Moving to tapping on his forearm, he felt energy flow to his big toe. He was so surprised and stated, "What does that mean?"

As I explained to him, it simply meant his energy flowed as it was intended to through the proper channels within him. He gained an inner awareness that, yes, there are softer, finer movements of energies within himself, moving to bring him to a higher place of being.

An EmoTrance Experience: Releasing Past Anger

Being a health professional, I have had occasions (I actually make them happen!) to share EmoTrance with several of the doctors with whom I come in contact. I had the opportunity to work with a doctor who had been experiencing deep anger over a situation that had occurred in his life.

This session brings out one of the greatest benefits to using EmoTrance. The doctor never had to speak of the situation that had caused the distress in his life. The issue remained private. The EmoTrance process worked strictly on his energy injury, which was the actual cause of his pain and stress. By the end of the session, the event or person which gave rise to the emotional injury no longer had an effect on the doctor; in fact, he was laughing as the session ended, thus leaving him transformed into a more joyful state of being.

This is a very different approach from counseling or therapy strategies of the past. If you have ever experienced counseling, as I have, the event leading to the emotional stress takes precedence and there is much discussion around the actual situation and not the location of the internal injury itself, or the *Energioso Stuckitis*.

With the information we know now, discussing an event over and over again may only add to the energetic block. This is a complete turn around in thinking. Working on the energetic block itself reveals an avenue of resolution! Research in the field of Energy Psychology has been very compelling in this direction.

This session with the doctor began with a brief description of what EmoTrance is and the importance of the energy system in healing. Fortunately, the doctor had a foundation in energy medicine (which was unusual because he was a surgeon coming from the traditional medical model), so little discussion was needed about energetic approaches to healing. After I gave him a brief description of EmoTrance, the doctor asked a few questions and we proceeded to this conversation:

"What do you like about EmoTrance?" he asked.

Happy to share, I replied, "EmoTrance has made me aware of the movement of energy, not only through my energy system, but my entire energy body. I never felt energy move before EmoTrance, although it was present. Before EmoTrance, I never realized that the tightness in my throat, for instance, was damage to my energy system and that something could be done about it! It has changed my life and I flow energy all the time now or at least as often as I can!" (I laughed).

"How do I know if I have damage to my energy system?" he asked.

"With EmoTrance you can identify the injury to the energy system through your emotions. If you are experiencing emotional pain, the location of that sensation identifies the injury or damage to your energy system or, as EmoTrance theorizes, to your entire energy body." I responded.

"Is it like Reiki?" he wondered.

"As you know, I am a Reiki Master and Reiki is another method for stress reduction and healing. I could use this whole session for a discussion of the differences between the two. Reiki involves the "laying on of hands" as you, the client, lies in a relaxed position, most likely on a massage table. There is little energy involvement on your part.

"EmoTrance is a very different modality and is based on practical research over many years. As you experience it in a few moments, you will find that it is a specific technique involving your experience of an energy blockage within *you*. It requires your total participation with guidance from the EmoTrance Practitioner. This is known as the 'client-practitioner dance'".

Satisfied with the response and now excited about EmoTrance, he said, "Alright, how do I go about learning EmoTrance?"

"EmoTrance stands for Emotional Transformation and is a modality that transforms the negative emotions of anger, fear, and agitation to emotions of joy, love and peace," I informed him. "Negative emotions create energy blockages and those energy blockages are the actual injury to the energy system. Are you aware of your energy system?"

"Yes, I know about it through acupuncture and other treatments. I haven't used them, but I know they exist. This sounds good, but how does it all work?" He was very curious.

"With EmoTrance, you identify the injury to the energy system through the emotions. Your emotions are your body's inner guidance system telling you the status of your energy body. As you learn to flow energy, you might even think it's your imagination (which is a whole other story), but you really are experiencing energy shifting and flowing in your body."

"I'm ready," he said with anticipation.

"First, let's find a situation in which you had heightened emotions. Is there a time you felt extremely angry about something or someone?" I said.

"Absolutely, got it." he said with certainty.

"Terrific. Think of that heightened energy situation and put yourself there as if it were happening now. Where do you feel that in your body?" I asked.

"Stomach," he declared.

"That is where the damage to your energy system is," I replied.

"Uh, OK." His eyes held a quizzical "aha" look.

"If you CAT scanned that spot, if you took an MRI or an x-ray, what results would you get back?" I quizzed.

"It would say there is nothing there."

"But you know there is something there, right? (He nodded) You feel it. In fact, where you 'feel' it is the exact location of the damage to your energy system. No guess work," I emphasized.

"Ok," he said. "Now what do you do about that?" He was really interested now.

"Think about the situation again. Where do you feel it your body? Show me with your hands."

He placed his hands over his stomach.

"On a scale from 1 to 10, how uncomfortable is the energy?" I asked.

"A 10." He stated.

"Put all your attention there and ask that the energy in that area to soften by saying, "Soften and flow."

After a pause, while I waited for him to ask the energy to soften, I said, "If the energy could leave, where would it want to go?"

"Where would it want to go?" he asked, unsure.

"Let's say the energy is as hard as ice in your abdomen area. Image the ice melting and the energy dripping away, starting to leave. Where would it go?"

"It feels like it is dissipating, I can't say where, but there is much less there," he thoughtfully responded.

"Great. So where the energy in your stomach was a 10 when we first started, what is it now? Continue to soften," I encouraged.

He paused, "It's a 3 or 4, definitely not like it was."

"Now place yourself in the situation again. Where do you feel it in your body?"

"Same place," he said.

"Is it a 3 or 4?"

"No, it's less now, maybe a 2," he said with a little wonder to his voice.

"The damage to your energy system is clearing. This modality addresses emotional sensations directly. I do not know of another system that does this so beautifully. It goes straight to the energy and works to move it again and clear the blockage. Do you agree?" I asked.

He nodded his head. I could see he was still experiencing the freedom of his recent transformation.

"No one has addressed this energy. It is your intention that makes it flow. It is not in your mind. The thought may be, but the energy is located in a blocked area. Your intention is the key to clearing the blockage. Your 'intention' to flow this blockage is what will get your energy to flow.

"Remember the adage, 'You become what you think about.' This is the same mindset. In the past, you and I have also discussed how 'thoughts become things, choose the good ones,' (tut.com). Your thoughts have become this energy lodged in your stomach. Your thoughts judged something to be good or bad and that created stuck energy."

"Right, I get that," he said.

"The EmoTrance modality views energy as just that—energy. It is only energy. All energy is meant to flow, no matter what you are doing. What has happened here is when you make a judgment, for example, "He's better than me..."

"Yes!" he interjected. "And that energy gets stuck right?"

"Right!" I agreed, happy he caught on quickly to the concept. "Making a negative judgment about someone or something starts to slow down the energy flow and is the beginning of a blockage to the energy system. On the other side of this thought, one of the things I have learned through EmoTrance is that if I am flowing energy and passing energy through me, I cannot be judging someone else at the same time."

"I get it," he said, with some seriousness.

"But I am jumping ahead with EmoTrance," I said. "The coolest thing is that you felt stuck energy and you felt energy move in you."

"Right," he agreed. "That was amazing."

"And through your intention, you felt it start to dissipate," I continued.

"Right," he nodded.

"OK," I said, "let's go back to the situation that is now a 2. The energy is still in your stomach? (he nodded) Now tell it to soften, soften and flow. Surround it with loving warmth and see it melting."

"That's weird," he opened his eyes. "I felt the energy move to my hands."

"Terrific! Now soften and flow the energy in your hands and have the energy flow out."

"OK," he said introspectively.

"Now let's go back to where you had a 10 energy in your stomach. What is it now?" I asked.

"Hardly anything," he said with excitement and a smile.

I smiled. "Let's revisit the original situation that caused the blockage and put yourself there again. This is how we test in EmoTrance to see if your energy is flowing and the blockage is cleared. Now that you are back in this angry situation, what are you on scale of 1 to 10?"

"Really I don't feel it anymore," he said with wonder.

"So you would say you are at a 0?" I asked.

"Yes," he said definitively.

"Well, in EmoTrance we are not done yet," I said.

"Really?" He was surprised.

I continued. "I know it is unusual to go beyond 0, even though that's the way we are instructed in our medical model. All we look at is the scale of 0 to 10. 10 is unbearable pain and 0 is no pain. We feel like we are done if people leave with simply no pain."

"That's right," he agreed.

"Well," I told him, "in EmoTrance there is a SUE scale meaning Subjective Units of Experience (refer to Figure 2, page 23). EmoTrance looks at 0 to a negative 10 for the level of emotional pain and 0 to plus 10 as a measure of how quickly the energy is flowing. This part of the scale indicates levels of joy, with total bliss being at the high end of the scale. Now, when you think of this situation, let's see if you can move to the other side of the scale where energy is flowing in a 'feel good' way. Think of the situation again. Where do you feel the energy?"

"In my hands, now," he said.

"Soften and flow," I guided.

"Ok, now there is less," he said thoughtfully.

"Shake out your hands," I encouraged.

"It's gone." he said.

"Now think of another aspect of the situation that created your anger. Where do you feel it in your body?"

"I don't feel anything," he said.

I continued. "Now, if it is hard to find the spot, but you do not feel you can move to the other side of the scale, there may be other aspects to the overall problem showing up. You may have shielded yourself against this and you just don't feel it in your body. Do you mind if we check that out?"

"No," he responded with curiosity.

"OK, when you think of the situation, put your arm up and picture the situation at the end of your arm. Is it an arm's distance away from your body?"

Surprised, he said, "That's too close to me. It's farther away than that."

"Good." (I stood up and started moving away to find the location of the shield.) Is it here? (he responded, "No") About here? (I moved back farther and he still responded, "No.") I continued to walk backwards until I was a couple of yards away from him, where he stopped me."

"OK, about there," he said.

"So, here's this bubble (I made a gesture indicating a bubble with my hands) and this whole situation is in this bubble. This bubble is going to travel towards you. Where do you feel it in your body as I take a few steps towards you?" I asked.

After about three steps he said, "In my hands."

"Soften and flow your hands. Where is the energy going? If the energy could leave, where would it want to go?" I asked.

"Where does it want to go?" he repeated. "...away, out."

"Good! So as I step closer, where do you feel it in your body?"

He laughed as he said, "My hands again."

"Great, soften and flow your hands," I encouraged him.

"Ok, it's gone," he reported.

"Let me move closer with this situation."

I moved towards him with the imaginary bubble in my hands. I stopped when he said, "I feel it in my hands again." He laughed with disbelief.

"Soften and flow that," I said.

"I don't feel it."

I stepped closer with the bubble until I was right next to him.

"I feel it again," he laughed again in disbelief. "Why is that?"

I responded, "We have created shields since our childhood to protect our delicate energy systems. Many times, as adults, we unknowingly hold onto these shields to continue to protect ourselves. But the shields are no longer needed and we our depriving ourselves of the energy nutrition we need to move on."

He nodded in agreement.

"Let's return to the shield," I said. "Now that I am near you, how far away is your situation?"

"Now it's about at arm's length." He smiled.

"Here is the shield." I make an imaginary shield with my hands. "Try to imagine a small pin prick of a hole in the shield. Where do you feel the energy coming through the shield in your body?"

"My hands again," he replied. Then he added in surprise, "It feels like it has gone to my feet!"

"Soften and flow," I said gently. "Can the energy flow out of your feet?"

"Yes, it's gone," he replied.

"Let's test if it's working. Here's the shield and there's a little larger pin hole of energy coming through. Where do you feel that in your body?"

"My feet," he said with a bit of a smile and shaking his head.

The doctor continued to soften and flow the energy as the hole in the imaginary shield became larger and larger, letting more of the situation's energy in. Finally, we came to a point where the hole was very large in the shield and I asked, "Where do you feel this in your body?"

He responded with a smile, "I don't feel anything."

I asked, "Can you dissolve the shield?"

"Yes," he smiled. "It doesn't matter anymore." He looked relaxed and his face looked younger.

I added, "So, now you have softened and flowed this situation through you and out into the universe and it no longer has control over you. (He nodded.) Once it had ownership over you but now you have evolved to where it does not."

"Keep flowing the energy through your body, keep rolling it through until you get a tingly sensation," I encouraged him. (He smiled.)

"There is an EmoTrance Activity called an Innocent Energy Shower. Finish up by imagining yourself showering with innocent energy in the form of light droplets of rain. (I paused). While you are in this shower, soften and flow."

The doctor responded enthusiastically to the innocent energy, "That's great...it's warming...That's amazing, sharp, that's cool."

The EmoTrance session ended and the doctor was grateful for the time spent learning this new modality.

Through the EmoTrance process, the doctor was able to release stress as he flowed the energies of anger and frustration concerning a situation he had kept private. He experienced complete relief and was laughing (a sign of the energized end state) at the end of the session. A follow-up call affirmed the success of the session as the doctor stated that EmoTrance had released the stress of anger he had been carrying with him for a period of time.

Time to Pause

Releasing Anger

- Is there a situation involving anger in your life that is causing undue stress in your body?
- Anger at another person is "a poison pill you give yourself", hoping that it may damage the other person. It is only hurting you, your physical body, your spirit and your energy system. It may be costing you too much to hold on to this anger.
- Forgiveness is so hard to achieve when your focus remains on the event or the individual instead of the *Energioso Stuckitis* or sensation of blocked energy. The energy sensation lodged within the body needs to be addressed and the EmoTrance process provides the relief needed.

No, that does not mean you have to forgive. It just means you are open to the possibility to forgive. This openness may be the initial flow of energy moving through your body that can initiate forgiveness and free you from the blockages of anger and hatred that can fester in your energy body, wreaking havoc on your spirit. The power of emotional transformation (EmoTrance) becomes apparent when the sensation of anger can be flowed into love and well-being!

- When performing this activity, try to stay focused on the sensation in your body, especially if the anger present is of a more recent occurrence. This may be difficult because of the close attachment the sensation has to the event. Speaking from experience, my mind wanders back to the person that is the focus of my anger and not the sensation itself. If this happens to you as well, be gentle with yourself. Acknowledge where you are in the healing process and continue on with EmoTrance, trying to stay centered on the emotion and its location in your body.
- Think of a time when you were angry.
- Where do you feel that in your body?
- Show yourself with your hands.
- How does the energy feel?
- Place your full attention there.
- Where else do you feel this in your body?
- If the energy could leave, where would it want to go?
- Say, "Soften and flow."
- Where does the energy want to go?
- Say, "Soften and flow."
- Continue the EmoTrance process until you reach a flow of energy that is tingly and energizing!

An EmoTrance Experience: Nurses and Their Desire to Know More

This story will give you a more in-depth understanding of the concepts of EmoTrance. These nurses quickly identified emotional pain and the location it took in their body. They also explored different aspects of stuck energy. EmoTrance and EmoTrance Tender Touch is demonstrated here as well.

An opportunity arose to discuss EmoTrance with four nurses at a social gathering. I did not know the group initially, but after telling them I was a physical therapist with an emphasis on stress management, the conversation opened up.

One of the nurses, Mary, told me of her intense nervousness about a neck massage she was to receive from a physical therapist the next day.

I brought up EmoTrance and how it is an incredible tool to use for emotional blocks and how it helps the energy system. They were all interested and wanted to know more about what EmoTrance was and wanted me to explain further with a demonstration.

"OK then," I agreed, "I want you all to think of an emotional issue that comes up for you. Something or someone you are angry at."

Looking around, I could tell by the expressions on their faces that they all could think of something. I asked each to gauge the emotion on a SUE scale of 0 to 10, 10 being highly emotionally painful and 0 being no pain.

Candice responded she was at an 8, Karen softly added a 5, Dana said an 8 and Mary stated that it was absolutely an 8.

I encouraged them to think and reflect as I asked, "Where do you feel this in your body? Where is the location?"

I looked around and saw some nodding, knowing they were experiencing something new, and said, "Show me with your hands."

Mary moved her hands to her stomach. Dana placed a hand on the back of her neck. Karen moved a hand over her heart and Candice placed both hands on her heart.

Their attention was directly on me as I told them, "Your hands are identifying stuck energy that is there inside of you. Think about it, that energy, the location of your emotional pain, is showing you the exact location of the injury to your energy system."

There were looks of interest and disbelief on the four faces.

"Just think," I said to open their inner awareness, "If you x-rayed that spot, took an MRI or a CAT scan, you would find there was nothing wrong with you. Do you agree?"

They slowly nodded as if that made sense.

"Yet, you know something is there, don't you?"

They all agreed.

"So that knot of energy..." I began

"Tenseness" someone added.

I continued, "...or solid feeling in you lets you know, without a doubt, that something is there. Do you agree?"

They nodded and I added, "That's stuck energy and energy needs to flow."

They all seemed intrigued and agreed somewhat.

"It's so noisy in here," said Karen. "Would it be better if we had a quieter place to do this technique?"

"It would be nice, of course, but, no, it's not necessary. And that is the beauty of EmoTrance! It's not meditation where you need a quiet place to go to for it to be effective. It's a modality you can use anywhere at any time to flow energy when you need to, not just when you have a good spot to do it in. You simply can intend energy to flow, anywhere you are and any situation you are in. It is a tool to ease emotional stress and bring more joy in your life, anytime you want to."

"That sounds great!" said Karen. "Tell me more."

I said, "Let's move on to the next step. Do you all remember the emotional pain that you identified in yourself?" They all nodded with extreme interest waiting for the next cue.

"Alright everyone, now ask that energy inside of you to soften, ask it to soften and flow."

When I received some quizzical looks, I added, "Let's say it's as hard as ice, warm it and feel it melting and dripping away. Feel the energy soften and flow. Think, where does the energy want to go? Let's ask Candice what is happening for her."

I turned to Candice and said, "Do you feel the energy softening?" She nodded. "Where is it going?"

"Down," she replied and lifted her hands from her heart and made a waving motion down towards her stomach and out into the air. "It seems to be moving from my heart to my stomach and out," she added.

I said to her, "Now on a scale of 0 to 10, what is your emotional pain now."

She said in surprise, "I don't feel it right now. It's gone." She thought for a moment and challenged, "But it's been gone before. That's how emotional pain happens. You get upset and after a while it just goes away on its own."

"Good point and we'll discuss that, but first, what about you Mary? Did you get a release?" She responded she was down to a 5. I questioned the others and Karen said she was a 2 and Dana said she was a 4. "Please notice that you all were able to flow energy and reduce your emotional discomfort."

"Let's discuss Candice's point," I said, going back to her statement. "Energy is meant to flow and not get stuck. Yet more often, when we have an emotional issue and it is painful, most likely we are not "flowing" it out, but storing it up somewhere. That's why it came back so clearly for you just now. You had it stored somewhere. It had never flowed out of you as a river flows out, emptying itself in the sea. The energy was stuck somewhere, stagnant, waiting to be addressed."

The others nodded in agreement, as did Candice with a smile.

"I like to make the analogy of Tupperware. We have all taken stored energy in the form of food, placed it in Tupperware, and put it in the fridge thinking we would get to it later. But let's say we don't get it later. What happens to it?

"It rots," says Dana emphatically.

I laughed, "Yes, when you finally get to it, it may be rotting. Now in the meantime you have put more stored energy in the form of food in the fridge in other Tupperware containers and they are all building up as well. When the door is closed and you forget about the containers, does that mean the situation is gone? Is all that stored food taking care of itself and going away on its own?"

There was some shaking of heads.

"Sure enough," I continued, "You go to look at the situation again and there is that old stored food, sometimes just ready to burst through its container."

"So, Candice, you may not be feeling the old emotional wound at times, but it is quite possible that it is sitting, rotting away somewhere in your system, just ready and waiting to come out and be taken care of."

"Look at Dana. When she thought of her emotionally painful situation and I asked where she felt it in her body, she pointed to her neck. Theoretically speaking, sooner or later that emotional energy in her neck may become more of a physical issue if it is not addressed. For example, Dana, if I asked you right now who was or is 'a pain in your neck', would you be able to come up with something?"

"Oh, right away," she said emphatically. She turned to the other nurses and stated in reassurance, "It's none of you though."

"Donna, do you have neck pain right now?"

"Yes" she said.

"Would you mind if I touched a spot on your neck?"

"I wouldn't mind at all!" she said expectantly, with a little hope attached.

I touched a point on her neck and asked, "What is this point on a scale of 0 to 10?"

"It hurts; that's about a 6 or 7," she responded.

"As I press here, is there anywhere else you feel this pain in your body?"

"No."

"Check your hands, feet, thighs, stomach, and head."

She responded no to all, but said, "Isn't that interesting because the pain is down to a 5."

"Terrific," I responded, "Now, say to the pain in the area I am pressing on and ask it to soften and flow. Where does the pain want to go?"

"It is going out where your finger is pressing. In fact it is gone! Can you believe that?" she said to the others who were watching intently. "The pain is gone!"

To emphasize my point I added, "Thus, energy is meant to flow, emotional energy is meant to flow and let me add that physical pain energy is meant to flow as well." Dana was still rotating her neck back and forth in disbelief that her pain was gone.

"What do you mean by, 'energy is meant to flow'?" said Karen, more curious than before.

"Everything is energy and energy is meant to flow. Let's take the energy of a single cell. It is constantly moving. If the cell became stagnant and stopped moving it would die and cease to exist." As nurses, they all agreed to that.

"Or take the circulatory system. Blood is meant to keep moving and flowing in the body. What would happen if the blood stopped flowing or simply stopped altogether and became stagnant? Oxygen exchange would deplete itself, cells would die, infection and then, depending on the extent of the stoppage, death."

"Well that was dramatic!" Dana laughed.

"My point is energy is meant to flow whether it is physical energy or emotional energy. It is meant to flow," I emphasized.

"Point made," said Dana, as others nodded in agreement.

"Why do you think we didn't realize all this sooner? It sounds so simple," Mary added.

"That question can take many different directions, but we were all trained in our professions in the medical model. The medical model is based on Newtonian physics, which looks at the body as a machine. The head, along with spirit and emotion, were placed elsewhere because a machine is not influenced by spirit and emotion. All the early medical books were written by men, with very little influence by women.

"Yet, you as nurses know that you can never separate the body from the mind and spirit. Now we are at a wonderful place in time to bring all this back together again in our healing professions."

They all agreed it was true. One of them asked, "But, would this be considered science?"

"All science starts with a good question, observations, and theories. That is what I am presenting to you here."

"I agree," said Karen. "Let's start bringing this information to our nursing students! I think everyone here would agree that we could use a seminar on EmoTrance!"

Time to Pause

Emotional Healing

- Have you ever had an emotion from a past situation that 'has gone away', but comes back when recalled?
- Pause and use the EmoTrance process to release the emotional energy involved.
- Dana had neck pain. Although EmoTrance is for emotional pain and release, you can experiment to see if you can use this process to reduce physical pain.*

The Tender Touch EmoTrance Technique

- Find a tender area in a muscle around your shoulder or neck area.
- Put pressure into that area until you feel a little discomfort.
- Rate the discomfort on a scale from 1 to 10 so that you can compare your results following EmoTrance to the area.
- Scan your body.
- Do you feel the tenderness or any traveling sensation anywhere else in your body? If you do, address that first and soften and flow those areas until the energy has flowed and dissipated.
- Go back to the point you are pressing. What would you rate that now?
- Say to the area, "Soften and flow."
- Where does the energy want to go?
- "Soften and flow."
- Repeat until the tenderness under your finger is gone.
- Pause
- What did you experience?

*This actual technique is called Inner Awareness Method, which is the application of EmoTrance to body work.

An EmoTrance Experience: A Sixth Grade Class: Math Test Anxiety and Problems with Bullies

EmoTrance is a perfect modality with children. Children tend to "get" the energy system flow of their body with little explanation. This may be because children can still experience the feeling of energy in their body and have not yet become oblivious to their own energy through the stressors and busy-ness our society makes us take on.

After presenting EmoTrance at a Parent–Teacher Association evening program, I was approached by a sixth-grade teacher who asked if I could teach her class this technique. She was worried about the level of stress in the classroom from two aspects—the first was the pressure the students were feeling as the exam for math placements was approaching and the second was the issue of *name calling* resulting from some bullying occurring outside the classroom.

I told the teacher I would be happy to do so and was given a special two-hour time frame to work with the children.

In the classroom, the children gathered in a circle around me, eager and attentive, although a bit wary of my presence. I explained to them that EmoTrance is a modality that helps to move stuck energy in the body and a hand immediately went up.

"What's stuck energy?" asked one of the boys, as the others giggled.

Well, I bet you already have experienced it!" I said, happy for the question. "Would you like to see if you have any?" I gestured for him to step forward.

With a nod of the head, he came to the center of the circle.

I turned to look at the other children and told them all to participate. As I asked their classmate questions I told them to do the same for themselves.

The young man's name was Craig. "Craig, is there anything that is bothering you or upsetting you lately?"

"Yeah," he said emphatically and with dread, "The math placement tests." There was a bit of a droning sound the other children made as they felt his pain.

I turned to the class and asked, "How many of you are stressed out about the math placement tests? Raise your hand." The entire class raised their hand.

"Think about a scale from 1 to 10, with 1 being calm and 10 being so stressed you can hardly bear it. I want you to close your eyes and raise your hand when I call out a number. If that is where you are in your stress level, raise your hand."

"How many are about a five?" I asked and no one raised their hands.

"How many are stressed to about a six?" There was one child who raised her hand.

"How many are stressed to about a seven?" Five children raised their hand.

"How many are stressed to about an eight?" Eight children raised their hand.

"How many of you are stressed to a nine?" Six children raised their hand.

"How many of you are stressed to a ten?" The last four raised their hand.

"Wow, this is a lot of stress for you all to have!" I said compassionately.

"Tell me about it," said Craig emphatically.

(I was shocked at the level of stress these children were experiencing. This is something we need to address in our schools on a larger scale!)

"OK everyone, you do this too. Craig, when I say 'math test' where do you feel that in your body?"

"In my stomach!" said Craig.

"Show me with your hands," I prompted him. Craig immediately placed his hands on his upper and lower abdomen area.

"OK everyone, show me with your hands were you feel 'math test' in your body. Wow, look around and notice that the majority of you feel it in your stomachs. Some of you feel it in your hearts, and the rest of you in your heads."

I looked at Craig and then at the others and said, "That is what stuck energy feels like."

"I have a lot of stuck energy then," Craig said, "Because I have been feeling this a lot lately." (Kids learn so quickly.)

"Would you like to get rid of it?" I asked the entire class and there were nods, and "sures" and a few "duhs".

I turned to Craig and asked, "What does the energy feel like in your stomach?"

"Butterflies," he replied.

I turned to ask one of the girls who had placed a hand on her heart, "And yours? How does your stuck energy feel?"

"It feels hard," she replied.

"As hard as ice?" I queried and she nodded. I turned to them all and said, "Think about how your energy feels to you. Is it hard like ice? Murky? Or looser like the butterflies Craig is experiencing? Find that for yourself. Now I want you to close your eyes and connect with that energy and ask it to soften, to soften and flow."

After they closed their eyes, I said gently, "Soften and flow. Where does the energy want to go? Craig, where does the energy want to go?"

"Down my leg and out," he said.

I asked a few others. "Where does the pain energy want to go?"

Some responses were, "out my hands," or "out my head," or "just straight out." One person said, "I don't know."

I turned to the one that said she didn't know and noticed she had her hand on her heart. I cued her to "soften and flow" and then asked, "Is there anywhere else you feel this in your body?"

"My throat" she responded, surprised.

"Good job," I told her. "You are doing great. So now continue to say in your mind, 'Soften and flow.' See if you can get that energy in your throat to soften."

When she nodded, I asked, "Where does it want to go?"

"Out my mouth," she responded, in a slightly surprised way.

"Good! Keep doing that. Everyone, continue to soften and flow and see where the energy wants to go and intend it to flow out." I turned to Craig. "How are you doing?"

"There is still some there, but not so much," he reported.

"You are all so good at this! Keep going, Craig, soften and flow."

"How many feel they got most of the stuck energy out?" a majority of hands went up.

"Let's try something different. Jump up and down and shake your hands and jiggle your energy around." There were a lot of smiles and the children had fun jumping.

"Keep going," I said. I waited a few more moments and clapped my hands and gave a stop signal. There was a lot of heavy breathing and many smiles.

"Now where do you feel the energy in your body?" One child raised her hand and responded, "All over!"

"That's right! All over. Energy is meant to flow and move all over and out!"

Checking in on Craig I asked, "How is your energy now?"

"Good" he said

"If I say 'math test', where do you feel that in your body?"

"I don't feel it right now," he said with a smile.

"Remember," I said to the whole class, "when you are feeling stressed, it is only energy! You can move that energy by asking yourself where you feel it in your body and asking it to soften and flow. If you have trouble with getting some to leave, move around, dance, take a walk, breathe deeply. Energy loves to move."

At this point, I decided to move on to the name-calling situation the children had been experiencing in the bullying situation. I asked each person to find a partner and told them we were going to use EmoTrance to help when someone called them a hurtful name.

I modeled the activity with their teacher first and asked her to call me a name. She couldn't do it because it "wasn't nice".

I laughed and let the children know she was right, but for the sake of the exercise, we needed to practice this.

I changed my approach and asked if I could have permission to insult her. Everyone laughed. I asked her what name I could call her. She said, "Ugly," and the class laughed again.

I said to her, "You are ugly." Her face turned a little red. "Where do you feel that in your body?"

"I feel it in my heart," she said.

I said, "Show me with your hands." She put a hand on her heart.

"Where else do you feel it in your body?" I asked.

"Just in my heart," she responded.

"How does the energy in your heart feel?" I asked.

"Hard and stuck," she responded.

"Soften and flow." I said, guiding the teacher through the EmoTrance process.

The teacher was able to clear the word "ugly" and we repeated the steps until we were all laughing. The teacher reported that the word now made her laugh.

After this example, we had the students practice. I asked the students what a hurtful word was for them and they responded, "idiot". With two student volunteers, I demonstrated how to use the EmoTrance process to clear the emotional pain of the word "idiot" until the two students that demonstrated the technique were laughing and the class was laughing.

As I left the children that day, I was overwhelmed with the need and the importance of bringing strategies to children to help them relieve their stress, fears, and worries, especially in the areas of exam stress and, for many, the fear of bullies.

I find with EmoTrance, in regard to bullies, that if children can be empowered to clear their emotional energy from hurtful words, there probably would not be any bullies because there would be no victims to be found.

Time to Pause

Relieving Stress

- These children experienced high levels of stress through their desire to perform well on their math placement tests.
- Where in your life do you feel high levels of stress?
- Maybe there is more than one.
- Pause
- Write down each and EmoTrance each one.
- What did you experience regarding the flow of energy within you?

Bullying

- When have you felt bullied in your life?

- List the names that hurt you and go to the "Insults" activity in Part III.
- For me, I need look no further than my own thoughts.
- I am amazed at how I can bully myself.
- Do you have thoughts that are negative or degrading?
- Pause
- Take time to write them down and see if you can EmoTrance them.

Closing

He came into my office angry and unsure. I do not know how the mother managed to get this teenager through my door! Billy did not like his teachers, he despised the sciences, and he hated going to school. At 15 years old, life was far from a happy experience for him.

"You are not going to make me like science," he challenged.

"You're right!" I responded. "But I am here to teach you about a cool technique that works with your body's energy."

After a little more explanation, I asked, "Just for a moment, think of your science teacher. Where do you feel that in your body?"

He turned inward and placed his hands on his solar plexus. He looked up quizzically.

"That right there, Billy, is damage to your energy system and you can do something about it." I paused looking intently at him. "Would you like to do something about that stuck energy?"

"Yeah," he replied with curiosity.

"Put all your attention on the energy under your hands and tell it to 'soften and flow...soften and flow'."

"Where is the energy moving?"

Down my legs." he replied with surprise.

"Great job," I responded. "You are learning a skill that no one else in your High School knows—how to release the sensation you have that is causing your discomfort. This sensation is only stuck energy. If you practice this technique, that painful sensation in your stomach area is going to dissipate and flow through your body and out."

"Sweet," he said, now fully engaged.

We continued on with the EmoTrance process until the energy was cleared and flowing. By the end of the session he was smiling and laughing at stories we were exchanging. As he left the office he said with a smile and a slight laugh that he would text me and let me know how many times he needed to soften and flow in science class the next day.

Emotional Transformation had taken place. He came in angry and left light-hearted with a smile on his face.

Before we parted, I asked if there was the one single most important idea he learned from our session today. He responded, "I never knew what I was feeling was stuck energy and that I could flow it. I can do something about it."

This is why I love EmoTrance. It is empowering and leaves both children and adults with a technique to change the way they view emotional energy. EmoTrance acknowledges the emotional sensation as stuck energy (*Energioso Stuckitis!*) and gives a simple modality to relieve that sensation, making life a more blissful place to be.

There are so many stressors in life. Without the tools to release the stuck energy of stress and flow it through the energy body, life can become unbearable.

EmoTrance gives you the ability to transform emotional pain surrounding your stress, to flow this *Energioso Stuckitis* and transform it to love and joy.

Although *Energioso Stuckitis* was a fun word I created to emphasize the issues surrounding stress in our lives, it brings to light the damaging effects of stress and the importance of using EmoTrance to flow the energies instead of allowing them to "get stuck".

As adults we may be experiencing many stressors, but I hope the case study of EmoTrance and the sixth grade class, along with Billy, emphasizes the stresses our children are experiencing at such young ages.

We Need EmoTrance

Our nervous system is constantly under attack. Even when the pressures outside ourselves are under control, our multimedia world and technology have overburdened us. In the past 100 years, information has increased astronomically. Our nervous systems were not designed to handle the constant assaults we receive every day. Our nervous systems have not caught up.

EmoTrance gives us the tool to flow energy and release the stresses that come our way. EmoTrance recognizes that our physical bodies were never meant to handle the stressors life presents, but our energy systems can. Our energy body is equipped with the ability to move energy through our systems quickly and efficiently when drawn on to do so.

Look around you. Very few people know that the relief to their stress and emotional pain lies within themselves, lies within the simple intention to just "soften and flow".

As you practice these techniques and enjoy the increased freedom that comes when your energy is flowing, I hope you will take these new tools and share them with others.

The ability to flow your own body's energies cannot be underestimated. It is a gift from the Creator and can awaken a remarkable tool for not only relieving stress, but for healing on a very deep and profound level. When healing happens, there is enhanced creativity, exploration, and adventure for life—the possibilities are endless.

A few hours after my meeting with Billy, I received this text:

"Hey, it's Billy. I just softened and flowed while doing my math homework and it worked!! Thought I'd let you know :)"

Billy's life was transformed with EmoTrance in a brief moment. Only time will tell how his life will continue to unfold.

Let us be a role model to not just Billy, but to children and adults alike. In a world of increasing stressors, let us show that it is possible to "soften and flow" and live a vibrant life filled with health, wealth, happiness and joy, utilizing a beautiful technique called EmoTrance!

REFERENCES AND RESOURCES

StressFish: De-Stress Online Fast

www.StressFish.com/

The EmoTrance Portal

www.EmoTrance.com/

DragonRising Publishing

www.DragonRising.com/

Dr Teresa Lynch: Official Website

www.TeresaLynch.com

Silvia Hartmann: Official Website

www.SilviaHartmann.com

Emotions and Feelings: Helping You Feel Better!

www.EmotionsandFeelings.com

The Association for Meridian and Energy Therapies

www.TheAMT.com

Aquarium Health

www.freshaquarium.about.com/od/termsandtables/a/aquariumhealth.htm

Diamond Alignment

www.diamondalignment.com

Tut's Adventurers Club

www.tut.com

Abraham Hicks

www.abraham-hicks.com

Sandra Hillawi

www.passionforhealth.com

Also in the *StressFishGuide to... Series*

The Stressfish Guide to Easy EFT by Silvia Hartmann

The StressFish Guide to Easy EFT by Dr. Silvia Hartmann is written to be the perfect introduction for beginners, but also has the effect of making seasoned professionals fall in love with the technique all over again!

Hartmann's unique, easy-to-read and fun writing style allows all readers of any age to pick up and learn the basics of what is often described as the "wonder technique".

Also from DragonRising Publishing

EmoTrance by Dr Silvia Hartmann
Emotions, Energy, Information and Love

This book reveals one of the most important things you can ever learn about how to keep mentally and emotionally secure. Developed by Dr Hartmann after intensive personal research into how our bodies work and knowlege built on a foundation through her study of NLP, Project Sanctuary, and Emotional Freedom Techniques EFT, she has taken the revolutionary new field of energy therapy to the next level. Once the EmoTrance technique is mastered, it is possible to deal with any issue that may arise painlessly and effectively. As issues are dealt with one by one, one emerges into a world of health and vigor, where the world is filled with energy and life.

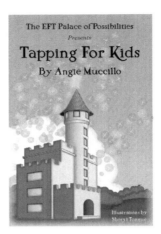

Tapping for Kids by Angie Muccillo
A Children's Guide To EFT Emotional Freedom Techniques

Tapping For Kids is an EFT children's book designed to teach 7–11-year-olds how to use EFT as a tool to help them overcome their fears, worries and everyday traumas, as well as build their self-esteem. *Tapping For Kids* is a perfect gift for all the children in your life!

Tapping for Kids is now in its second, full-colour edition that brings the story to life and captures children's imagination whilst they learn EFT. In addition, *Tapping for Kids* now comes with a audio CD that is not available anywhere else. It is packed full of read-along raps and rhymes to help your child learn. You'll also be given a link to download posters and certificates to make the experience unforgettable.

Adventures In EFT by Dr Silvia Hartmann

If you love EFT, then you will love *Adventures In EFT* by Dr Silvia Hartmann.

For five years, Silvia took EFT around the world and treated clients, friends, family, strangers in the street, on TV and callers on radio programmes for every possible human problem under the sun!

Her experiences and what she learned not just about EFT, but about how people really work and what has to be done to change their experiences of life make simply fascinating reading for professionals and lay people alike.

With in-depth examples and step-by-step guides on how to use EFT for weight loss, addictions, sex, money, relationships, children, test anxiety, phobias, sport performance, traumatic memories and much, much more, Adventures in EFT in it's sixth revised edition is an absolute "must have" for anyone who loves EFT!

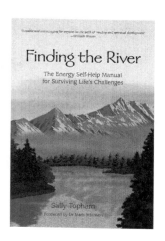

Finding the River by Sally Topham
The Energy Self-Help Guide for Surviving Life's Challenges

Life can be a struggle, this is a fact, both work and personal life are full of their ups and downs. Energy Therapies are some of the simplest and most effective methods of combating life's challenges, but even so, just finding the right Therapy for you can be a struggle in its self.

Finding the River by Sally Topham is a compendium of self-help exercises and techniques from a vast array of Energy Therapies, and is designed to help a person cope with life's many challenges, find inner peace and feel a comforting sense of connection between oneself and the natural world.

Excel at Sports by Jimmy Petruzzi

Be the Best at Sports, Business and Life with NLP

Elite athletes know that there is as little as 1% difference between being the best, and being at the back of the field.

Excel at Sports by Jimmy Petruzzi is a simple, concise and ground-breaking guide to NLP Neuro Linguistic Programming and other techniques that can give you that extra 1%, whether in sports, business or life in general.

From professional athletes competing on the world stage, to pub league players, we all like to perform at our best. Excel at Sport is for athletes, amateurs, coaches and teachers, anyone who wants to know what it takes to be the best. The techniques in this book can be used in all aspects of life, from on the sports field to a high-pressure business meeting, from pushing yourself in the gym to making the most of family life.

About the Author

Dr. Teresa Lynch is passionate about helping people live life to the fullest. Coming from a life which has presented many personal challenges, she has searched for ways to bring her spirit to a place of health, wealth and well-being.

Dr. Lynch's introduction to the world of healing began with a Bachelor's Degree in Physical Therapy followed by a Master's in Health Sciences, both attained from Stony Brook University, Long Island, New York. Finally Dr. Lynch received a transitional Doctorate in Physical Therapy from Thomas Jefferson University in Philadelphia, Pennsylvania.

After being diagnosed with a major debilitating illness, Dr. Lynch went on to explore alternative ways for healing and attained an Alternative Graduate Degree in Advanced Massage from Health Choices Massage School in Belle Mead, New Jersey. Taking time off to raise children, she began a small business, Healing to Wellness, which today has expanded to offer EmoTrance and other Energy Therapies.

Dr. Lynch lives in Belle Mead, New Jersey, is married and has four children. She enjoys teaching, and along with maintaining her private practice, is presently an Assistant Professor at Union County College in Plainfield, New Jersey teaching Physical Therapy.

Online Stress Relief With the StressFish

Quick Stress Tips, Anti-Stress Methods,
Online Stress Relief Techniques and More...

De-stress online fast with The StressFish!

www.StressFish.com